SAN FRANCISCO'S
CELEBRITY
CHEFS

Sponsored by

THE
MONTEREY VINEYARD®

Sam Bronfman and The San Francisco Ballet

PEANUT BUTTER PUBLISHING

PEANUT BUTTER PUBLISHING
SEATTLE, WASHINGTON

First Printing—January, 1987
10 9 8 7 6 5 4 3 2

Peanut Butter Publishing
329 - 2nd Avenue W.
Seattle, WA 98119

ISBN 0-89716-164-5

CONTENTS

22, AVENUE D'EYLAU, 75116 PARIS (FRANCE) · TEL. (1) 45 05 13 73 · TELEX 630 468

PIERRE SALINGER
BUREAU CHIEF

It was more than 30 years ago. I was prowling
the streets of San Francisco looking for little
tidbits of information to fill the columns of Bob de Roos
in The Chronicle. Herb Caen had left us for
The Examiner. Of course, I knew he hated it and he
would come back, but there had to be a Caen-line column,
so I had been designated as Bob's street man and that
meant making the tours of San Francisco's best
restaurants and cafes.

One advantage of this assignment was that one ate
and drank well. At lunch time, you had to swing by
Jack's, one of the city's best fish restaurants. The
real estate tycoon, Louis Lurie, was always at the
table where he ate for 50 years, surrounded by the
San Francisco elite. Or it was up to Telegraph Hill
and Julius Castle, where the quality of the food matched
the stunning view of San Francisco Bay. In the late
afternoon, always to the foot of Hyde Street, where
through the special influence of Stan Delaplane, the
best bartenders from Dublin had installed Irish Coffee.
At night, it was always at Bimbo's, a restaurant and
night-club, specializing in fat steaks and baked potatoes.

The advantage of San Francisco, as a culinary
capital, has always been linked up to its international
character. Whether you wanted a great French, Italian,
German, Spanish, Mexican, Polynesian, Greek, or Chinese
meal, it was almost at your doorstep. That is why
San Franciscans understand good gastronomy, and why
this book opens our eyes to all kinds of recipes and
suggestions that could only originate in San Francisco.

I am pleased to share these reminiscences for the
benefit of the San Francisco Ballet and my native city.

Pierre Salinger

From the time I moved to Northern California and joined the wine business in 1979, I have enjoyed this beautiful area of the world. The mere mention of the Bay Area evokes a wonderful image of wine country, great restaurants, beautiful golf courses, the spectacular coastline and, of course, fog!

It is a real pleasure to have been invited to co-author this historic collection of recipes, especially for such a worthwhile cause. The San Francisco Ballet is the oldest and one of the finest in the country and deserves the support of the entire community.

Many thanks for your continued interest in fine wine, fine food and the arts, all of which add so much to the quality of life for which the San Francisco area is well-renowned. We at The Monterey Vineyard, Domaine Mumm and Sterling Vineyards are proud to be part of this community.

Sam Bronfman II
President,
Seagram Classics Wine Company

SAN FRANCISCO CELEBRITY CHEFS

SAN FRANCISCO BALLET

455 Franklin Street San Francisco. California 94102 (415) 861-5600 Writer's direct line:

Helgi Tomasson
Artistic Director

Richard L. Cammack
School Director

Richard E. LeBlond, Jr.
President. Chief Executive Officer

Timothy Duncan
General Manager. Assistant to the President

San Francisco Ballet, the oldest classical ballet company in the United States, is proud of its exemplary tradition of firsts. The Company gave its premiere performance in 1933 and has since grown to a company of international stature with a history and profile unique in American dance.

The incomparable quality which characterizes San Francisco Ballet is spawned from a fusion of the Continental Classical traditions with an instinctive American spirit. There is an indefatigable dynamism which inspires the Company. This is fueled by a dedication to producing superior performances of classical and contemporary ballet and to providing the highest caliber of training for dancers aspiring to professional careers.

In a pioneering move to support this ideal, the San Francisco Ballet Association built the first comprehensive facility ever created to house a major dance institution. With the support of our generous community, the Association constructed one of the finest, most modern ballet training and rehearsal spaces in the country.

This past December, San Francisco Ballet unveiled a spectacular new production of Nutcracker. The Company presented the Western World's first complete performance of the Christmas classic in 1944. The San Francisco Ballet Association offered $1.5 million of 5% Subordinated Debentures due in 1996 to finance the new Nutcracker, a funding approach which had never before been used by a not-for-profit performing arts institution. With this innovative financing program, San Francisco Ballet again demonstrated its ability to blend artistic creativity with administrative innovation.

Through our performances and projects such as San Francisco's Celebrity Chefs, the San Francisco Ballet Association strives to entertain and to enrich life in our community.

Timothy Duncan
General Manager

"CELEBRITY CHEF SPECIAL"

A unique mixture of the finest ingredients, blended well, with a resulting flavor we hope you will enjoy.

COMBINE:
- 1 Generous portion THE MONTEREY VINEYARD
- 1 Innovative PEANUT BUTTER PUBLISHER

ADD:
- 1 Active Auxiliary
- 1 Compulsive Chairman
- 1 Marketing Master
- 1 Peerless Pierre Salinger
- 1 Excellent Editor
- 1 Department of Developers
- 1 Benevolent Board of Trustees

MIX:
- 205 Creative CELEBRITY CHEFS
- Magnums of Enthusiasm
- Heaping Scoop of Support
- Sophisticated Seasoning
- Zest of San Francisco

FINAL PREPARATION:

Thoroughly assemble all ingredients.

Quickly pour into publishing house.

Gently remove from printers.

Eagerly spread into the community.

SERVES: ABSOLUTELY EVERYONE!

Linda Plant

ACKNOWLEDGEMENTS

Special thanks to all the celebrities who shared their favorite recipes with us.

Many thanks to members of the San Francisco Ballet Auxiliary who worked so hard to make this book a success:

Linda Plant, Chairwoman, whose leadership was invaluable.

Auxiliary members: Ingrid Weiss, President; Deborah Rabin, Public Relations; Jola Anderson, Vera Carpeneti, Nini Dibble, Jane Flahaven, Dixie Furlong, Jean Grayson, Janet Grosser, Belinda Lowenthal, Patricia Marcucci, Christa Revnes, Diana Stone, Dormi Willis, and Ruth Wilson.

Special thanks to Edward Plant, John Anderson and Morton Grosser.

San Francisco Ballet Association; Christine Dohrmann and Christine Seaver.

Gary Ibsen of The Monterey Vineyard.

Gordon Swanson of Windward Design for production.

Elaine Lotzkar for editing.

Concept Color.

The San Francisco Ballet Auxiliary wishes to thank Samuel Bronfman, II, President of Seagram Classics Wine Co., and George T.D. Sandeman, Product Manager, for their extreme generosity and help without which this project would not have become a reality.

ANSEL ADAMS

ROUTE 1, BOX 181, CARMEL, CALIFORNIA 93923   TELEPHONE (408) 624-2558

The American Southwest, and specifically New Mexico, has been a favorite destination for both Ansel and myself. Our first visits were in the late 1920's and over the years we found many reasons to return. Ansel photographed extensively in Chimayo, outside of Santa Fe, at the wonderful adobe Santuario. I discovered the power and subtlety of New Mexican red chile during one of our trips. Chimayo chile has the reputation for being the very best, and our old friend and photographic historian Beaumont Newhall has kept me well supplied in recent years.

Photographable Chicken

4 boneless chicken breasts
Salt and pepper to taste
1 T. corn oil & 1 T. butter
1 can Tomatillos
1 cup heavy cream

2 large, ripe tomatoes
¼ cup finely chopped red onion
1 t. Chimayo chile
1 finely chopped small clove garlic
1 T. fresh lime juice
Chopped cilantro

Place each chicken breast between two pieces of wax paper and pound gently with flat wooden mallet to thin.
Heat oil and butter in skillet until sizzling.
Cook seasoned chicken breasts until just done and lightly browned - approximately three minutes per side.

Spoon pool of tomatillo sauce on warmed plate. Place chicken breast on sauce, artfully top with fresh salsa and sprinkle with chopped cilantro.

Tomatillo Sauce: Place Tomatillos in blender or food processor - liquify. Add tomatillos to heavy cream. Heat but do not boil.

Fresh salsa: Peel and chop tomatoes. Stir in red onions, Chimayo chile, chopped garlic and fresh lime juice. Let mellow at room temperature for a couple of hours before using.

Virginia Adams

Robert M. Adams, M.D.
A PROFESSIONAL CORPORATION
966 Cass Street, Suite 200
Monterey, California 93940
(408) 649-1144

CRABMEAT NEW ORLEANS STYLE

DELICIOUS FIRST COURSE APPETIZER
(SERVES 6-8)

1 LARGE PACKAGE OF PHILADELPHIA CREAM CHEESE
1 STICK OF BUTTER
1 POUND OF WHITE CRABMEAT
1 SMALL FINELY CHOPPED ONION
5 CLOVES OF GARLIC (MINCED)
1/8 TEASPOON OF TABASCO SAUCE
DASH OF CAYENNE PEPPER
8 THIN SLICES OF BREAD (BUTTERED)
2 LEMONS
PARSLEY

IN A DOUBLE BOILER, MELT THE CREAM CHEESE AND BUTTER. ADD CRABMEAT AND SEASONING. HEAT THROUGH. SERVE OVER TOASTED BREAD THAT HAS HAD THE CRUST CUT OFF AND CUT IN TRIANGLES. GARNISH WITH SLICED LEMON AND PARSLEY.

THIS IS SUCH A QUICK AND EASY RECIPE BUT OH- SO DELICIOUS. IT TAKES US BACK TO OUR MOST FAVORITE RESTAURANT CITY IN ALL OF THE UNITED STATES.

BOB AND DONNA ADAMS

Bob and Donna

KURT HERBERT ADLER
GENERAL DIRECTOR EMERITUS
SAN FRANCISCO OPERA

VANILLEKIPFERL
(Vanilla Crescents)

Ingredients:

1 cup, less 2 tablespoons butter
2-1/2 cups all purpose flour
1/2 cup sugar
1/2 cup blanched almonds, ground
2 egg yolks
1/2 teaspoon vanilla
powdered sugar

Cut the cold butter into 2-1/2 cups of flour sifted with 1/2 cup of sugar. Add 1/2 cup almonds, the egg yolks, and the vanilla and work the ingredients into a smooth dough. Chill dough for at least 1 hour. Roll into strips about the thickness of a finger and cut the strips into two inch pieces. Roll out each piece until it is three inches long and curve it into a crescent. Bake in slow oven (300° F.) on a buttered baking sheet for about 20 minutes until cookies are dry and slightly colored. Sprinkle a plate heavily with powdered sugar. With a spatula transfer cookies to the plate and sprinkle with more powdered sugar.

A delicate after dinner cookie which goes well with fruit or sherbet.

Makes about forty.

B∧ Bank of America

K A S H A. . . . . . .Made Perfect

Every year on January 1, we surround ourselves with good friends,
good food and good cheer. To add to the festive mood I always
make this marvelous ethnic side dish....with always enough left-
over.

1 egg
1 cup kasha
1/4 cup margarine
1 cup chopped onion
1 cup chopped celery
2 cups warm chicken broth
1/4 tsp. ground ginger
1/4 tsp. dry mustard
salt

Combine the egg and kasha in a small bowl and set aside; saute
onion and celery in margarine in a large skillet. When tender,
add kasha and stir over medium heat until each grain is separate.
Add hot chicken broth, ginger, dry mustard; cover pan tightly and
simmer for 15 minutes or until liquid is absorbed and grains are
tender.

If you wish you may add bow-tie noodles (cooked); bell peppers,
mushrooms...be creative!

This is an excellent stuffing for turkey and/or chicken.

Deanna R. Adolph
Manager

Bank of America National Trust and Savings Association
Seventh and Mission Streets   Carmel, California 93921

4

Pasta alla Siciliana

For 8 servings

3 pounds fresh, ripe plum
    tomatoes
1/2 cup olive oil
1 cup finely chopped
    yellow onions
6 whole cloves garlic, peeled
1 teaspoon salt

1 teaspoon white pepper
Melanzane alla Sis
Fresh basil leaves
Pasta of your choice
    (rigatoni ours)
Freshly grated Parmesan

1. Wash the tomatoes in cold water. Gently dry them. Cut them in quarters and place in a stock pot with chopped onions and whole garlic cloves. Drizzle the olive oil on top. Uncovered, simmer gently for 1-1/2 hours, stirring occasionally.

2. Remove and discard the garlic. Puree the tomatoes through a food mill into a saucepan. Discard the seeds and skin.

3. Return the sauce to stove and simmer until it reaches the consistency you desire. (This depends upon you and your tomatoes.) Season to taste with salt, pepper and olive oil.

4. Mix in the **Melanzane alla Sis**, saving some slices to put on the top of your pasta. (Sauce will keep and be even tastier in a day.) Immediately before serving, add fresh basil leaves.

5. Cook your pasta until firm but tender, al dente. Drain until dry. Add a pat of butter and toss. Gently fold in sauce.

6. Place on hot plates. Garnish with additional sauce, basil, Melanzane and Parmesan.

Melanzane alla Sis

3 - 4 shiny eggplants
Salt

Olive oil for drizzling
Freshly ground pepper

1. Wash and pat dry eggplants.

2. Cut them waistwise in half inch slices. Set the slices across pasta colander and sprinkle with salt. Layer it and sprinkle more salt. Weight the colander with a heavy plate and let eggplant drain for two hours. Dry eggplant well with paper towels.

3. Put in broiler pan, sprinkle with pepper and drizzle with olive oil.

4. Broil at 500 degrees Fahrenheit until golden brown on each side. Drain on paper towels.

Sicilian Purists say "NO!" but for our feast alla San Francisco we also include freshly grated parmesan, hot sourdough bread, salad, a California Cabernet and figs for dessert followed by expresso with Vin Santo and biscotti!

Joseph L. Alioto

DOLORES & 6TH • CARMEL

Bud Allen opened his famous Irish, English and American "It's Buds Pub" in Carmel November of 1984.

While offering traditional Pub fare, Bud sought to make certain dishes unique to his establishment. Bud worked closely with Chef John Money, sharing ideas to create "Bud's Own Corned Beef Shepherds Pie."

BUD'S OWN CORNED BEEF SHEPHERDS PIE

1/8 tsp Ground Thyme	1/8 tsp Ground Bay Leaves
1/2 tsp Ground Marjoram	1/2 tsp Ground Coriander
1/2 tsp Salt	1 Qt. Heavy Cream
2 Drops Tabasco Sauce	2 Drops Maggi Seasoning
3 Cups Mashed Potatoes	1 Bunch Green Onions- finely chopped

2 TBS Soft Butter and 2TBS Flour kneaded together

1 Bell Pepper, 1 Red Bell Pepper, & 1 Med White Onion - Julienne and Par Boil.

1 & 1/2 lbs Corned Beef - Cooked and diced.*

* Reserve the juice that Corned Beef is cooked in to thin filling if needed.

PIE FILLING:

Heat cream and add all seasonings. Whisk well and simmer 15-20 mins, stirring often. Gradually whisk in Butter/Flour mixture until sauce is smooth. Add Corned Beef and simmer sauce for another 10 minutes. Sauce should have a stew-like consistency.

ASSEMBLY:

Coat the bottom of a deep, oven proof casserole dish with melted butter. Alternately layer pie filling and pepper mixture in casserole. Using a pastry bag, pipe the mashed potatoes evenly over the top of the casserole. Dribble clarified butter over the potatoes and bake at 425° for 30-35 minutes or until golden brown and crisp.

Serves 6 - 8.

ENJOY!

Bud

H.E. "Bud" Allen

MOUSSE AU CHOCOLAT A L'ORANGE
ten to twelve servings

1	teaspoon unsweetened cocoa
1	teaspoon instant coffee, preferably expresso
¼	cup boiling water
7	ounces chocolate (6 ounces semisweet and 1 ounce bitter, or 3 ounces sweet and 4 ounces bitter)
4	tablespoons sweet butter, cut into pieces
4	eggs separated
3/4	cup superfine sugar
3	tablespoons Grand Marnier or other orange-flavored liqueur
	Grated rind of 1 orange
1	cup heavy whipping cream
½	teaspoon salt

Must be prepared at least 4 hours in advance, even better when made 24 hours in advance.

Dissolve cocoa and instant coffee in boiling water and pour into top of double boiler. Add chocolate and melt over simmering water. Then add butter, bit by bit, beating with wire whisk till each piece is incorporated.

In mixing bowl, beat egg yolks and sugar with electric beater till light yellow and thick. Add chocolate mixture, continuing to beat. Then beat in Grand Marnier and grated rind. Beat 1/2 cup of cream till thick, and fold in. Beat egg whites and salt till stiff, then fold in very carefully.

Pour into a serving bowl (I use a cut crystal bowl so the chocolate shows through) or individual serving glasses. Chill for at least 4 hours before serving. Mousse will have a better texture if chilled in a cool place but not in the refrigerator.

Just before serving, beat remaining 1/2 cup of cream, and line circumference of serving bowl, or glasses.

Gene Andrews

Eugeunia R. Andrews,
President

DURNEY
VINEYARD

A Wine Estate
Carmel Valley

ARTICHOKE OLE'

FROM MONTEREY COUNTY, THE ARTICHOKE
CAPITAL OF THE WORLD!

INGREDIENTS:

2 Jars (6 oz.) - Marinated Artichoke Hearts
1 Can (4 oz.) - Diced Mild Ortega Green Chiles
              - Mayonnaise
              - Cheddar Cheese (Mild)

Drain the Artichoke Hearts and puree in blender
with the diced chiles.

Place the puree in an ungreased quiche dish.
Cover with mayonnaise, then grate enough
cheddar cheese to cover the mayonnaise.

Heat through at 325°F oven just long enough
to melt the cheese. Serve warm with tortilla
chips.

**   This recipe is easy, fast, delicious and
     always has received rave reviews.

BY: *Christine Durney Armanasco*
CHRISTINE DURNEY ARMANASCO

Business Office • P.O. Box 222016 • Carmel, California 93922 • (408) 625-5433

LOIN OF VEAL WITH SUN DRIED TOMATO DUXELL, WHOLE GRAIN MUSTARD SAUCE

ONE	LOIN OF VEAL, WELL TRIMMED
24	MUSHROOMS, FINE DICED
3 TABLESP.	SHALLOTS
4 OZ.	SUN DRIED TOMATOES, FINELY DICED: NO OIL
4 OZ.	PORT WINE

SALT AND PEPPER TO TASTE

SAUCE –

BEEF & VEAL BONES. MAKE A STOCK (½ GALLON) AND REDUCE TO 1/3, ADD DASH OF PORT
AND SWIRL IN POMMERY WHOLE GRAIN MUSTARD TO TASTE. ADD SOUR CREAM TO TASTE
AND ADJUST SEASONING.

METHOD –

WITH A CLEAN STEEL, POKE A HOLE LENGTHWISE THROUGH THE LOIN. FILL WITH
DUXELL & SUN DRIED TOMATO MIXTURE. TO MAKE, SAUTE SHALLOTS AND ADD MUSHROOMS
AND SUN DRIED TOMATOES. REDUCE TILL THERE IS NO LIQUID. ADD PORT WINE AND REDUCE
AGAIN UNTIL THERE IS NO LIQUID. ADD SALT & PEPPER TO TASTE & COOL. SEAR OFF
VEAL LOIN AND FINISH IN THE OVEN AT 375 UNTIL INTERNAL TEMPERATURE IS 132 F.
LET REST 20 MINUTES & SLICE TO ORDER.

TWO SLICES PER PERSON. YIELD 8 PEOPLE.

C.E.C.

Executive Chef.

B abette

2343 Third St. #230
San Francisco, CA 94107
(415) 621-2343

RAINY DAY PASTA FOR TWO

½ POUND PASTA COOKED AL DENTE

5 TOES FRESH GARLIC CHOPPED

2 TABLESPOONS OF GOOD OLIVE OIL

1 TABLESPOON BUTTER

½ BASKET CHERRY TOMATOES CUT IN HALF

¼ CUP CHOPPED FLAT LEAF PARSLEY

FRESH GROUND PEPPER
COARSE GROUND SALT

SAUTE GARLIC IN OLIVE OIL + BUTTER UNTIL COOKED BUT NOT BURNT, TOSS IN TOMATOES + WARM BRIEFLY, POUR OVER PASTA + TOSS WITH PARSLEY, SALT + PEPPER. ENJOY!

Enrico's Restaurant
504 Broadway
San Francisco
392-6220

The idea of Angel Wings came from my grandmother. Always
the secret of her pastas or raviolis was the thinness and "al dente"
cooking of them. After making the raviolis she used to take the
leftover pasta cutting it into irregular squares and boiling it.
With a touch of Bolognese Sauce, as a child, to me it was the closest
thing to heaven on my palate. Thus the name Angel Wings came about
recalling my childhood memories. Today I've elaborated upon that
basic dish by adding either spinach, basil or avocado to the dough
and cutting them into uniform squares. I personally prefer a touch
of Bolognese, a little butter and cheese, but whatever the sauce
chosen, marinara or white, or just butter and cheese, it is definitely
a heavenly taste treat.

AVOCADO ANGEL WINGS with SAUCE FLORENTINA

Put $3\frac{1}{2}$ cups of all-purpose flour and 1/8 teaspoon salt in a large
mixing bowl. In a small bowl mash 1 very ripe avocado and mix it
thoroughly with 3 medium eggs. Combine the avocado mixture and flour
and mix completely smooth in a food processor or electric mixer. If
necessary add a tablespoon or two of water to get a kneadable dough.
Turn the dough onto a floured slab or board and knead by hand for
5 to 7 minutes. The avocado will make the dough extremely soft.
Roll it into paper-thin sheets, either with pasta machine or by rolling
it out between sheets of waxed paper. Cut the dough into $1\frac{1}{2}$-inch
squares and stack them, three at a time, between waxed paper.
Place on board or cookie sheet and chill in the freezer for $\frac{1}{2}$ to 3/4
hour, until firm. Remove, drop the squares into a large pot of
rapidly boiling water and cook about 3 minutes, until "al dente"
or just firm to the bite. Drain the pasta and put back in the pot
leaving at least 8-10 teaspoons of water in the pot. Add salt and
pepper to taste, 2 tablespoons soft butter, 2 chopped very ripe
avocados, 2 cups of heavy cream and 2 to 3 tablespoons Parmesan Cheese.
Stir very gently over medium heat, then transfer to a serving dish,
sprinkle with a little more Parmesan and serve at once. It will
serve 6 as a main course or more as a first course.

JO BARTON

Spinach and Artichoke Casserole

1 tall can artichoke hearts or, better yet, 3 fresh
artichoke hearts, sliced into 6 pieces

2 packages frozen spinach, finely chopped, or
better yet, 4 packages of fresh spinach
stemmed, steamed and finely chopped

1 cup medium white sauce made with 2T butter,
3T flour and 1 cup milk

1/3 cup freshly grated Parmesan cheese

1 handful bread crumbs

Place artichoke hearts in a 1 quart pyrex
buttered casserole. Spread the spinach, that
has been carefully squeezed to eliminate any
moisture, over the artichokes. Top with the
white sauce and the cheese and a few bread
crumbs. Dot with butter and place in a 350
degree oven for twenty minutes or until
lightly brown and bubbly.

Serves six but is easy to double for twelve.

This is an old family recipe that we enjoy
every Thanksgiving. It does take time to wash
and steam all that spinach but it is well
worth it. This can also be done the day
before and baked just before dinner. I hope
you enjoy.

Jo Barton

Scott Beach
Actor, Broadcaster, Writer

BEACH'S BEEF JERKY

I invented this recipe after the lamentable and untimely demise of a company that used to make the best beef jerky on the market. With no sense of modesty at all, I claim that my recipe's even better than theirs. The problem is that you can't make enough of it to keep ahead of poachers, moochers, and other low forms of life. I advise that you make two batches at a time, and vehemently deny the existence of the one you hide.

INGREDIENTS

Flank steak

Soy or tamari sauce

Garlic powder

Curry powder

Wright's Liquid Smoke

Dry red wine

Ground black pepper

PROCEDURE

When you buy a flank steak, there's usually some visible fat on it. If your butcher can't take the trouble to trim it off, then you've got to do the job. Use a thin, sharp knife, and pretend you're a great surgeon as you remove that pesky fat.

Cut the meat into strips...with the grain...roughly a quarter-inch thick.

Now, make the marinade. There should be just enough to moisten the meat all over without leaving it dripping. Pour about a third of a cup of soy or tamari sauce in a bowl. Add a generous shaking of garlic powder (Lowry's coarse garlic powder is great!)...a hefty pinch of curry powder...four drops only! of Wright's Liquid Smoke...a slosh of red wine...and some ground black pepper, say about one Tbsp. Stir those items to mix 'em, and put your meat strips into the bowl and get them moist with the marinade. Cover the bottom of your oven with a sheet of foil to catch drips. Arrange the strips of marinated meat on the oven-rack. Heat the oven to 350 degrees and let the meat cook for 30 or 40 minutes. Then, turn the heat down to its lowest setting, and go write someone a love-letter in iambic pentameter for four hours. When you come back, you'll have yourself a batch of delicious beef jerky. Serves one, if you keep it out of sight.

Scott Beach

13

1264 ½ S.

Beverly Glen Blvd.

Los Angeles

CA 90024

Supremes de Volaille au Champagne
Chicken Breasts in Champagne Sauce

1/4 cup flour	1 lb. mushrooms, sliced
Salt, pepper	1 1/2 cups heavy cream
1/2 cup butter	1/4 - 3/8 cup champagne
Chicken breasts, boned (4)	

1. Remove skin and bones of Chicken breasts.

2. Mix 1/4 cup flour, 1 tsp. salt, 1/2 tsp. pepper; roll chicken in it.

3. Heat 1/2 cup butter in large skillet. Lightly brown chicken breasts.

4. Add 1 lb. mushrooms, sliced. Cover and cook 10 minutes. Transfer chicken and mushrooms and clean pan of all butter.

5. Return chicken and mushrooms to pan and add 1-1/2 cups cream and simmer over low heat 10 minutes.

6. Transfer breasts to warm serving dish.

7. SAUCE: Add to liquid in skillet--1/4 cup champagne. Bring to rapid boil and cook until sauce is reduced to a creamy consistency.

8. If you want sauce to thicken, add 1 - 2 Tbls. corn starch or arrowroot that has been mixed with a little of the sauce.

SERVE ON HEATED PLATES

SERVES 4

LIA TRIFF BELLI

November 15, 1986

One of my favorite recipes is:

APRICOT SOUFFLE

6 cup, well-buttered souffle dish
1 1/2 cups cooked, dried apricots
1/2 cup sugar
3 tbs. butter
3 tbs. flour

3/4 cup milk
4 egg yolks
2 tbs. apricot brandy
7 egg whites

Preheat oven to 375 degrees F. Sprinkle buttered souffle dish with a little sugar. Tie band of buttered waxed paper around top of dish to extend sides. Force apricots through fine sieve to yield 1 cup puree. Mix with 1/4 cup sugar. Set aside to cool. Melt butter in saucepan. Remove from heat. Stir in flour. Gradually blend in milk and remaining sugar. Stir over moderate heat until sauce barely begins to thicken. Remove from heat. Beat in egg yolks, one at a time. Add cooled puree and brandy. Beat egg whites until stiff, but not dry. Fold into apricot base. Fill prepared dish with souffle mixture. Bake in preheated oven 17-20 minutes or until well-puffed and risen, but still wobbles when lightly shaken.

Sincerely,

Lia Belli

Mrs. Melvin Belli

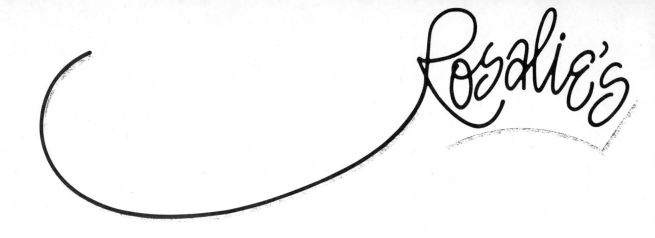

Special recipes always bring back special memories. This Gingersnap recipe was given to me at least 25 years ago by Mrs. Berg. I knew Mrs. Berg when she was probably about 63, selling hosiery at Weinstein's department store on Market Street. She, in my memory, was the ultimate Mother/Grandmother. She loved and nurtured both her children and grandchildren and often baked them:

GINGERSNAPS

Five dozen cookies
Preheat oven to 350 degrees

INGREDIENTS

3 cups sugar
2 1/4 cups shortening
3 eggs
3/4 cup molasses
1 tbl. cinnamon
1 tbl. cloves
1 tbl. ginger
4 1/2 cups flour
2 tbl. baking soda
1 1/2 tsp. salt

Mix well in one bowl. Form into balls the size of small walnuts and roll in sugar. Bake for 12 to 15 minutes. DO NOT OVERBAKE.

Bill Bellali

I don't have a favorite recipe, but here's one I like a lot.

CHICKEN BREASTS WITH LEEKS AND ORANGE

2 half chicken breasts
Sweet butter
3 leeks
Dry vermouth *as needed*
Juice 1 orange
1/2 teaspoon orange zest
Salt, pepper to taste

Remove skin and fat from chicken breasts and bone. Clean leeks and slice whites and some green into rounds. Zest and juice orange. Melt a little butter in a heavy saute pan and turn in chicken, meaty side down. Add leeks and cook until golden and translucent. Turn chicken. Add vermouth, orange zest and juice and salt and pepper to taste and cook, covered, turning the chicken a few times, until done, about 15 to 20 minutes.

Serve chicken, meaty side up, on a bed of steamed mixed-grain rice with the leeks and pan juices poured over all. Serves 2.

JANE BENET
Food Editor

VEAL CASSEROLE

2 egg yolks beaten with ½ cup light cream
¼ lb. salt pork, diced   1 green pepper, thinly sliced
3 T. olive oil   2 cups sliced mushrooms
1 medium onion, sliced   ½ cup dried apricots, chopped
1 clove garlic minced   1½ cups consomme
3 lbs. lean veal, cut in 2" cubes   3 T. lemon juice
2 T. fresh rosemary   ¼ cup dry marsala wine
3 tomatoes peeled and sliced   ¼ cup beurre manié *

Parboil the diced salt pork for 5 minutes. Drain.
Heat 3 T. olive oil in a heavy pot and add the sliced onion,
garlic and drained salt pork. When golden brown, add veal
cubes and sear quickly. Sprinkle with rosemary. Add tomatoes
green pepper, mushrooms, apricots, consomme, lemon juice
and wine.

Simmer over low heat until tender, about 1¼-1½ hours. Set
aside to cool. (*) May be done ahead to this point.

About 15 minutes before serving, remove meat from sauce.
Add the ¼ cup beurre manié to the sauce and cook about 8
minutes till sauce thickens, stirring constantly with a
wooden spoon. Return meat to pan and heat.

Blend egg yolks and cream in bowl with wire whip. Beat in
by spoonfuls 1 cup of the hot sauce. Then pour the mixture
into the pot with veal, blending the rest of the sauce with
the egg yolk mixture. Set over moderate heat for a few
minutes, but do not let it come to the simmer.

                              Serves 6

* Equal parts flour and butter mixed together.

In the evening, after the last guest had left, and after we
had tucked our staff into bed upstairs,...our staff being
daughters Suzanne, Janine, and Lucie, and our 10 year old
sous chef son, Daniel,...my wife and I would sit in front of
the fireplace in our now strangely quiet restaurant and reflect
upon the day. I would open a good bottle of wine, and we
would snack on pâté and cheese, or perhaps quiche, or soufflé,
or a rich, warm soup. Sorrel is a green, lemony, leafy vegetable that grows year round in Pacific Grove's sandy soil.
Often our midnight tête-à-tête supper would be hearty bowls of
sorrel soup, the sorrel fresh from our garden, along with
hunks of crusty French bread, and lots of love and laughter.
I share this recipe because it is so simple, and so good
either hot or cold, and because sorrel soup will always remind
me of the time when we all lived and worked together under the
protective old Victorian Maison Bergerac roof.

     Sorrel Soup   Soupe à l'oseille

4 bunches sorrel (approx. ½ lb.)   3 Tbsp. butter
6 white potatoes, diced   8 cups chicken stock
2 leeks, white only   ½ pt. heavy cream

Sauté potatoes, chopped leek and sorrel in butter. Add stock
and simmer until soft, about 1 hour. Put through food mill,
add cream, season with salt and pepper, reheat, (or chill, for
cold soup) and serve.

Raymond Bergerac

LYNN L. BERGERON
President

TRADER VIC'S
20 Cosmo Place
San Francisco, California 94109
415-775-6300

TRADER VIC'S

TAMUIN SALAD

INGREDIENTS:

½ Avocado, semi-ripe, peeled
1 Small Tomato, Semi-ripe, peeled
1 Green Pickled Jalapeno Pepper, chopped very fine
1 Level Tblsp. Onion, chopped very fine
2 Tblsp. Celery, chopped fine
¼ tsp. freshly ground Pepper
½ tsp. Salt
¼ small-ladle French Dressing
½ Cup Bay Shrimps
1 Head Lettuce Leaf
¼ Lemon

METHOD:

Dice avocado into ¼" squares. Dice tomato into
1/8" squares. Marinate shrimp in French dressing.
Mix above ingredients in salad bowl with the
exception of shrimp and lettuce leaf. Mix thoroughly
but lightly. Add a bit of lemon juice to the mixture.

Place lettuce leaf on chilled dinner plate. In the
bottom of a soup bowl, place the shrimps, then fill
with the salad mixture. Place the balance of the
salad mixture on the lettuce on the serving plate
and unmold the soup bowl.

Garnish with 4 spears of asparagus evenly around
the mound of salad and 4 slices of hard-cooked
eggs with one slice of black olive on each, evenly
in between the bottom ends of the asparagus.

Lynn L. Bergeron
President

Mailing Address: Post Office Box 2343, San Francisco, California 94126

:CHEZ:PANISSE:
:: CAFE:&:RESTAURANT ::
:: 1517:SHATTUCK:BERKELEY:94709 ::
:: 598·5525 ::

Roger Bertolli

Garlic-Baked Squid

Serves 2

8 whole fresh squids, approximately 5 inches long, cleaned and de-beaked

4 cloves garlic, thinly sliced

1 tablespoon extra virgin olive oil

1 tablespoon red wine

1 tablespoon chopped fresh parsley

1/2 cup aioli (garlic mayonnaise)

Preheat the oven to 500° F. Put the squid, including tentacles, in a bowl. Toss it with the garlic, olive oil and red wine. Arrange the squid on a sheet pan, pouring any wine, garlic and olive oil left in the bowl over it. Salt and pepper both sides lightly.

Bake the squid for 5 minutes. When done, transfer the squid to a warm plate. Collect the juice in the pan and add the chopped parsley to it. Arrange the squid on two plates. pour half the juice over each and serve with aioli and warm bread.

WAPPO HILL PEARS
(for four to six)

4 to 6 nice ripe pears but not soft or bruised.
(Bartlett, Comice, d'Anjou, Bosc)
Peel, leaving stems intact. Core with potato peeler
from bottom.

Poach pears in one bottle of Pinot Noir in a straight-sided
casserole, to which you have added:
3/4 cup of sugar
Juice of half a lemon: add some zest to the taste
1 stick of cinnamon
4 thin slices of fresh ginger

Poach for about 20 minutes, test for doneness with a fork.
Take pears out of liquid and cool them standing upright.
Reduce liquid to 1/2 cup.

In a small saucepan melt 8 oz. of good quality bitter
chocolate (semisweet if you prefer a sweeter dessert)
with 4 Tablespoons of heavy cream over low heat.

To Prepare

Coat dessert plate with the reduced Pinot Noir pear
liquid which is now quite syrupy.
Stand pear in the middle of the plate and dribble
some melted chocolate sauce over it.

A dab of whipping cream on the side with a small
mint leaf for garnish is optional.

MARGRIT BIEVER

BREAST OF PHEASANT
Capped with a morel cream sauce

Ingredients:

2½lbs (approx) pheasant
Morel mushrooms
onion, celery, carrot chopped
shallots (finely diced)
½ & ½
Clarified butter (2 parts) Oil (1 part)
Cognac
juniper berries
peppercorns
bay leaf
salt & pepper
flour for dusting

Method:

stock: cut up pheasant to obtain two boneless half breasts
and set aside. Cut off wings at first joint, cut off
drumsticks, take the bone out of the thigh. Save the thigh
meat for another use. In a medium small saucepan, brown
the pheasant carcass and bones. Add chopped onion, celery
and carrot to sweat with lid on for five minutes. Cover with
cold water, bring to the boil and reduce to one fifth. Strain
and set aside.

pheasant breasts and morel sauce:

fresh morels: soak in salt water 3-5 mins to kill
any worms, then rinse and drain.
dried morels: put morels in dish and add water to
reconstitute, drain.

Salt & pepper the breasts and dust with flour. In a hot saute
pan heat clarified butter and oil. Place breasts in pan,
skin side down until crisp and brown. Turn breasts over,
add chopped shallots and morels until meat is seared and
flavor is extracted from shallots and morels. Flame with
cognac and remove breasts. Add stock to pan and reduce to
a glaze. Add ½ & ½ and reduce to thicken. Return breasts
to pan to warm. Serves 2

Tips: Pheasant meat should have a crispy skin and pink meat.
      Do not overcook or it will become very tough.

 PS. I got this recipe from the owner of Night Bird Game Company;
Gerald cooked this meal for me on our first date(he attempted to
feed me rattle snake aux figues de Barbarie..No way.)
Well the pheasant was so good I married the guy..

Raquel Bitton

HANS BRANDT

As far as I know beef tartar originated in the eastern countries
of Europe, in the cold northern countries where people needed
a lot of protein to fight against the elements. The horsemen put
raw beef under their saddles, and as they rode, the beef became
tenderized. At their destination there was no fuel for cooking, so
they spiced the beef and ate it raw. Through years of civilization,
the formula of beef tartar has become more civilized, more refined.
It is still a speciality in nortnern countries like Denmark and
Germany. I am very fond of steak tartar, since I hate to cook.

Beef Tartar

6 ounces beef filet, completely trimmed of fat, and ground.
1 glass cup of each: finely minced fresh onions; finely minced
   anchovy filets; finely chopped fresh parsley; drained capers.
1 egg yolk, all chalaza removed.
fresh cut lemons
oil
brandy
Worcestershire sauce
black pepper
salt
watercress sprigs

Place a round serving plate in freezer to chill well. Place the
ground beef in the center of a large silver pedestal platter.
Shape it into a mound and score lightly with two dinner knives to
give the beef the appearance of having been chopped, not ground.
have the other ingediants ready. Lift the meat into a shallow
wooden salad bowl. Squeeze the juice of about ½ lemon on
the meat; sprinkle with a little brandy; sprinkle liberally with
Worcestershire.Grind on plenty of black pepper. Sprinkle with
about 4 teaspoons onions, 1 teaspoon anchovies. Add egg yolk.
Sprinkle with about 2 teaspoons parsley. Sprinkle with about 4
teaspoons capers. Salt to taste. Using two large spoons,
lightly, but thoroughly, mix all ingredients together. Lift
mixture into center of chilled serving plate. Using two dinner
knives, shape mixture into 4 inch square. Using the knives and
a light chopping motion, present it so its looks chopped and
lifted. Garnish with watercress, leaving plenty of white plate
showing. Serve with toasted thin slices of rye bread. Provide
salt, pepper grinder, additional cut lemons and Worcestershire
sauce for eater to add to taste. Makes one serving

Hans Brandt

SEAGRAM VINTNERS
375 PARK AVENUE
NEW YORK, NY 10152
(212) 572-1313

SAM BRONFMAN II
PRESIDENT

CRANBERRY CASSIS

(Adapted from a recipe by Martha Stewart)

3 cups fresh whole cranberries, crushed or ground in food processor

3 cups granulated white sugar

2 750ml bottles The Monterey Vineyard Chardonnay

Blend all together in a large bowl, stirring until sugar completely dissolves.

Spoon into sterilized canning jars.

Store 3 weeks in the refrigerator.

To serve, strain liquid directly into decanter or cordial glasses.

Crushed cranberries can be served over vanilla ice cream.

I often find myself pouring the cassis and the crushed cranberries over the ice cream.

Sam

EMBARCADERO CENTER

JAMES R. BRONKEMA
President and Managing General Partner

DELICIOUS SAN FRANCISCO CIOPPINO

2 tablespoons olive or salad oil
1 large onion, diced
1 large green pepper, diced
1 garlic clove, minced
2 28-ounce cans tomatoes
1/2 cup dry white wine
1/4 cup minced parsley
2 teaspoons salt
1/2 teaspoon basil
1/4 teaspoon coarsely ground black pepper
1 bay leaf
2 dozen littleneck clams
11/2 pounds Dungeness crab
1 pound fresh shelled and deveined shrimp
1 pound fresh scallops
1 pound fresh cod fillets, cut into
  2-inch chunks

ABOUT 45 MINUTES BEFORE SERVING:

In 8-quart Dutch oven or saucepot over medium heat, in hot
olive or salad oil, cook onion, green pepper, and garlic
until tender, stirring occasionally. Add tomatoes and their
liquid, wine, parsley, salt, basil, black pepper, and bay
leaf; heat to boiling. Reduce heat to low; cover and simmer
15 minutes.

Increase heat to medium-high; add clams; cook 10 minutes,
stirring occasionally. Add crab, shrimp, scallops, and cod
fillets and continue cooking 5 minutes longer or until clam
shells are open, shrimp turn pink, scallops lose their
transparency, and fish flakes easily when tested with fork.
Discard bay leaf. Serve in soup bowls with forks and
spoons. Makes 8 main-dish servings.

ENJOY! Jim Bronkema

Embarcadero Center, Ltd., A California Limited Partnership
Four Embarcadero Center, Suite 2600, San Francisco, CA 94111 (415) 772-0500

BAVARIAN APPLE TORTE

1/2 cup butter
1/3 cup sugar
1 tsp. vanilla
1 cup flour

Cream butter, sugar and vanilla. Blend in flour. Spread dough onto bottom and 1/4" up the sides of a 9" or 10" spring form pan.

2-8oz. pkg. cream cheese
1/2 cup sugar
2 eggs
1 tsp. vanilla

Combine softened cream cheese and sugar; mix well. Blend in egg and vanilla. Pour into pastry lined pan.

4 cups peeled and sliced tart apples
1/3 cup sugar
1/2 tsp. cinnamon

Mix sliced apples with sugar and cinnamon. Spread apples on cream cheese mixture. Bake at 450°, 10 minutes, reduce heat to 400° for 25 minutes longer or until knife inserted in center comes out clean. Enjoy!

This is an old family recipe brought over from Germany by my mother in law

CALIFORNIA STATE ASSEMBLY

WILLIE L. BROWN, JR.
SPEAKER OF THE ASSEMBLY

November 13, 1986

Linda Plant
Celebrity Chefs
San Francisco Ballet .
650 California Street
San Francisco, CA 94108

Dear Linda:

I can't cook!

Sincerely,

WILLIE LEWIS BROWN, JR.
Speaker of the Assembly

wlb/cc

SACRAMENTO OFFICE/STATE CAPITOL, SACRAMENTO, CALIFORNIA 95814   TELEPHONE (916) 445-8077
DISTRICT OFFICE/540 VAN NESS AVENUE, SAN FRANCISCO, CA 94102   TELEPHONE (415) 557-0784
NOT PRINTED OR MAILED AT PUBLIC EXPENSE

NIVEN BUSCH • 2625 BAKER STREET • SAN FRANCISCO • 94123

WILD JUNIPER TROUT

The first step in preparing this delicious dish is to make sure you tie on just the right fly and then flick it out like the dying breath of a saint to land just upstream of the ripple left in the smooth face of the stream by a rising 8 ounce trout. Failing the above, of course, you can go to a good market, for today the once mushy and tasteless hatchery fish foisted on the unwary buyer as trout have been replaced by speckled beauties raised in cold water and fed vitamin tested foods so that they come to the buyer almost as joyously as game specimens. Bone the little devil's flesh (white flesh okay, but if you have pink then we're dealing with a baby salmon or a steelhead, even better). Place 1 teaspoon margarine, and 1 teaspoon olive oil in pan. Heat so that touch of trout's tail makes a sizzle. Baste both sides of trout lightly with oil you lift from pan, then add six or seven crushed juniper berries to oil, drop trout in pan. While down side is cooking, sprinkle upside with cornmeal. In two or three minutes turn him over, sprinkle again with cornmeal, cook another minute, trying not to let the butter and oil brown. Garnish with the juniper berries. Serve. You now have a royal dish with the memory of pine forests and tumbling rapids in each delectable forkful.

Niven Busch

San Francisco Office
Four Embarcadero Center
Suite 3520
San Francisco, CA 94111
Telephone (415) 421-3110
Fax (415) 421-3128
Telex 176991 KPC&B

General Partners
Brook H. Byers
Frank J. Caufield
L. John Doerr
Thomas J. Perkins

Palo Alto Office
Two Embarcadero Place
2200 Geng Road
Palo Alto, CA 94303
Telephone (415) 424-1660
Fax (415) 856-2760

General Partners
E. Floyd Kvamme
James P. Lally

Consultant
Eugene Kleiner

CAMEMBERT OR BRIE SAUTÉ
HOT HORS D'OEUVRES

Dip a round of <u>Camembert</u> or <u>Brie</u> first in <u>1 beaten egg</u> then in <u>1 cup breadcrumbs</u>, then sauté in <u>1-2 tbs. butter</u> over medium heat until brown and crisp on both sides. Remove and keep warm. To the pan add <u>1-2 tbs. butter</u> and <u>¼ cup chopped chives</u> (or the green part of green onions) and sauté a moment or two, then pour over cheese. Serve with <u>water crackers.</u> (This can be garnished with a tomato rose.)

<u>Background:</u> In 1977 a friend persuaded me to take cooking lessons at Tante Marie's new school, especially since I could only cook breakfast. This recipe has endured as a quick but appreciated contribution to entertaining at home. As for the lessons, my fellow students tactfully voted me "most improved". At least my final exam wasn't burnt!

Brook Byers

30

RAISIN' CAEN SPAGHETTI SAUCE

2 Tablespoons Olive Oil
2 Tablespoons Unsalted Butter
2 Cloves of Garlic - Minced
3/4 Cups of Chopped Onions
4 Large Tomatoes - Seeded
2 Teaspoons Oregano
1 Teaspoon Nutmeg
Salt & Pepper to taste
3 Tablespoons Grated Parmesan Cheese
3 Tablespoons Fresh Parsley - Chopped
3 Dashes of Tabasco Sauce

In a heavy skillet...saute garlic and onion in
olive oil and butter for five minutes...add tomatoes,
oregano, nutmeg, salt, pepper and tabasco...cook
for 5 minutes...stir in parsley and parmesan cheese
and cook for 1 minute.

Serve immediately over your favorite pasta.

...Maybe with some nice, warm Herb bread and a salad.

*Good luck! you eat this at your own risk ...
Onward,
Herb Caen*

JOHN CALORI

CIMA ALA GENOVESE

STUFFED BREAST OF VEAL

Ingredients:

1 - 5 to 7 lb. Breast of Veal

For the Stuffing:

    1/2 lb. Ground Veal
    1/2 lb. Sweet Italian Sausage
      3 Bunches of Spinach
      1 Large Onion
      6 Cloves of Garlic
  1-1½ Cups of freshly grated Parmigiano
      1 Bunch of Parsley
    1½ Cups Bread Stuffing
      6 Eggs
      1 Cup Chicken Broth
    1/2 Cup Extra Virgin Olive Oil
       Fresh Italian Herb Mixture (Rosemary, Basil, Marjoram, Thyme, and Sage)
       Salt and Pepper
       Pinch of Nutmeg
      3 Hard Boiled Eggs

To Prepare the Stuffing:

Blanch spinach in large pot of boiling water, drain into colander, and let cool. Press out as much liquid as possible then chop coarsely. Transfer to a large mixing bowl and set aside. (If you wish, you can avoid the above by using frozen chopped spinach; thaw and drain well; be sure to press out as much liquid as possible.)

Chop onions, parsley, and garlic. Saute onions and garlic for about 5 minutes in olive oil. Add parsley and stir. Transfer to mixing bowl with spinach.

Saute veal and sausage meat (remove casing). Crumble and add to spinach mixture. Add bread stuffing and mix well.

Add parmigiano, herb mixture, nutmeg, and salt and pepper to taste. Mix well; add warmed chicken stock.

In a small bowl, whip 6 eggs. Add to stuffing; mixing thoroughly.

Place 1/2 the stuffing in the veal pocket. Then add the 3 hard cooked eggs in a row lengthwise down the center. Carefully, spoon remaining stuffing mix around and over the eggs, keeping them in place.

Sew up the end of the pocket with a needle and thread. Using your hands, roll the flat stuffed pocket until it resembles a loaf of bread. Then wrap and tie with string.

Place on a baking tray, massage the top with extra virgin olive oil. Salt and pepper (optional).

Bake in 300 degree oven for 1½ to 2 hours. (Top will be crusty and golden brown.)

When cooked, remove the breast and place on clean baking tray or jelly roll pan and cover with a weight of at least 10 lbs. (A slab of marble or a chopping board with books on top will do well.) Let it cool to room temperature for 4 to 6 hours. Transfer to refrigerator with weight still in place for at least 8 hours or up to 5 days before using.

Unwrap the cima and slice into slices of less than ½ inch thick. Best served at room temperature.

When trying to write a recipe which has been handed down, but never written down, it is difficult to give exact quantities. So experiment with the herbs, cheese, and garlic to suit your taste.

Cima, sliced tomatoes with mozzarella cheese and fresh Basil vinaigrette, figs, and a bottle of Cabernet makes a delightful cold supper for after the ballet.

John Calori

CAMERON and COMPANY • Publishers
543 Howard Street • San Francisco, California 94105 • 415/777-5582

No-Trouble Veal Casserole

Serves 8

This is so simple to make and exceptionally good. Guests can always taste the wine and sour cream, but there's an elusive herb they just can't identify. (Ed.)

3 pounds veal, cut for stew
1 medium onion, chopped
½ cup slivered almonds
½ teaspoon rosemary
½ teaspoon marjoram
1 can cream of chicken soup

Put meat in large shallow casserole, and sprinkle with onion, almonds and herbs. Spread undiluted soup over the top. Cover and bake 1 hour at 300°; reduce temperature to 250° and continue baking for about 2 hours. One pleasing feature of this recipe (in addition to its goodness) is that there is no browning of the meat; just put the ingredients together and bake it. Check occasionally during the last hour to make sure mixture has enough moisture. If it's getting dry, add a little water. If it seems too thin, remove cover. If dinner is to be delayed, turn heat very low.

BUICH BROS.
PROPRIETORS

SCALLOPS SAUTE A LA CANEPA
(Recipe for 2)

18 medium scallops
1 tbsp. flour
2 tbsp. olive oil
4 oz. butter
3 tbsp. chopped onion
pinch of salt
pinch of cayenne pepper
pinch of nutmeg
2 oz. chardonnay or chablis
6 oz. whipping cream

½ cup sour cream
1 tbsp. chives
1 tsp. chopped parsley
juice from 1 lemon

Drain scallops. Dust well with flour.

In saute skillet, heat oil and 2 oz. butter to medium temperature. Add scallops, cooking and turning them until lightly browned.
Add chopped onion, salt, cayenne pepper, and nutmeg; cook and stir
for 2 minutes. Add wine and cook to reduce wine. Add whipping
cream and cook for 4 minutes. Remove from heat.

Stir in sour cream, chives, chopped parsley, 2 oz. solid
butter, and lemon juice.

Serve immediately with buttered noodles and vegetables.

CHEF JOHN CANEPA

ESTABLISHED 1849

Joe Carcione
The Greengrocer ®

FRESH FRUITS & VEGETABLES   IMPORT-EXPORT-BROKER   RADIO-TV-AUTHOR-COLUMNIST

NEOPOLITAN TOMATO SAUCE

12 fresh tomatoes
4 cloves garlic
1 medium white or yellow onion

1 bay leaf
3 tbsp. olive oil or
    salad oil
salt and pepper

This delicious, all purpose sauce is the foundation of all good Italian cooking - for spaghetti, vegetable dishes, or casseroles. Blend 12 fresh tomatoes in electric blender until juice forms. Pour juice into saucepan and bring to boil. Then reduce to a slow simmer. Meanwhile, heat 3 tablespoons of oil in the frying pan. Slice 4 cloves of garlic and saute slowly in the oil until golden brown. Pour hot tomato juice into garlic mixture, then add 1 sliced onion, one bay leaf and salt and pepper to taste.

For spaghetti sauce, simmer slowly for one hour. For vegetable dishes, simmer for about 15 minutes, then add your favorite vegetable - zucchini, carrots, peas, beans, eggplant, or even hearts of artichokes - and continue cooking until tender. Sauce may be stored in refrigerator or frozen for use as needed.

The above is my favorite recipe, because I can still remember, when I was a little boy, standing by my Father as he cooked up this sauce. To this day, my wife and I make and keep several containers of this sauce in the freezer for surprise guests and unexpected dinners.

Joe Carcione
The Greengrocer

TELEX 331433 ● PHONE (415) 583-0319 or 761-4059 ● 53 GOLDEN GATE PRODUCE TERMINAL, SOUTH SAN FRANCISCO, CA. 94080 U.S.A.

36

Kitchens are allergic to me. Something horrible always happens, like 2½ minute eggs, or burned water. However, the following recipe always turns out perfectly. Enjoy.

OSSO BUCCO

Lightly flour 9 veal shanks, 1"-2" thick. Brown in 6 tblsp. margerine, careful to see that cut side is up, to prevent loss of marrow. Put in baking dish in 3 cups chicken broth, and add 1½ to 2 cups tomatoes, fresh or canned. Add 3 finely chopped garlic cloves. Cook at 325 until tender, 1-1½ hours. Fork meat to see if done.

Just before serving sprinkle with chopped parsely and the grated rind of at least 2 lemons.

Serve with Risotto Milanese.

the mandarin

900 North Point
Ghirardelli Square
San Francisco. CA 94109
(415) 673-8812

CRISPY CHICKEN SALAD
(serves 4 - 6)

Ingredients # 1:

```
1   3 lb. fryer
1/2 head of iceberg lettuce, shredded
3   scallions (white part only), shredded
1   C. rice sticks,  deep fried and broken up.  (The rice sticks
       are purchased dried and should  be dropped in hot oil  for
       only  about 3 seconds.  They also expand 2 to 3 times  in
       size, so use it sparingly.
1   C. fresh coriander, chopped with base of stems removed
1/2 C. peanuts and/or cashews, crushed
2   t. sesame seeds, toasted
```

Ingredients # 2:

```
4   T. water  chestnut powder (if unavailable,  cornstarch can be
       substituted,  but  water  chestnut powder  will  make  the
       chicken more crisp)
```

Seasoning # 1:   ## Seasoning # 2

```
1/4 C. warm salad oil                1 t. sesame oil
 2  t. Coleman's hot mustard
 1  t. salt
 1  t. sesame oil
1/2 t. five spice powder
```

Preparation:

Steam the fryer for 20 minutes or poach in slowly boiling water
for about 20 minutes. While the chicken is cooking, do all the
necessary shredding, chopping and crushing for the other
ingredients.

Let the chicken cool for 15 minutes and dust the outside with
water chestnut powder or cornstarch and steam for 5 minutes.
Cut the chicken in half along the backbone and make incisions
behind the wings and legs, then deep fry in hot oil for 10
minutes, until chicken is golden brown.

Bone the chicken and cut the meat into strips, 2 inches long and
about as thick as a pencil.

Combine the seasonings in a large mixing bowl and add the
chicken. Make sure the seasoning coats most of the chicken, then
add all the other ingredients except for the rice sticks. Toss
thoroughly. Add the rice sticks and seasoning # 2. Toss some
more to blend the flavors and serve.

                                        CECILIA CHANG

JOANIE CHAR

" Creamy Rice Pudding with Fruit "

Ingredients:

3/4	cup	rice
1	qt.	whole milk
3	Tbl.	sugar
2	tsp.	vanilla

1 1/2	cups	whipping cream (heavy)
3	Tbl.	confectioner's sugar
2	tsp.	vanilla
1/2	cup	apricot preserves (fine quality)
1/2	cup	red raspberry preserves (fine quality)

Directions:

Cook rice in milk at lowest possible heat, covered, until almost all liquid is absorbed, stirring often. Stir in sugar and add 2 teaspoons of vanilla, and set aside, covered, for several hours to cool. You can refrigerate for a day if you like. At this time, all milk will be absorbed by the rice and will have a slightly creamy texture.

Whip the cream and add confectioner's sugar and vanilla. Layer 1/3 of the rice, apricot preserves, and 1/3 of cream into crystal bowl or into individual dessert glasses. Spread preserves all the way to the edges, for the colorful layered effect. Layer another 1/3 cup of rice, all the raspberry preserves and 1/3 cup cream. Finish with a layer of rice, topped with cream.

Refrigerate for several hours before serving. This is a wonderful dessert or a delightfully decadent snack for any occasion. My friends and I have tried several variations and have always returned to the true recipe.

Enjoy,

Joanie Char

Joanie Char

MONTEREY BEACH HOTEL
2600 SAND DUNES DRIVE • MONTEREY, CALIFORNIA 93940 • (408) 394-3321

C A V I A R   M O U S S E

Empty 1 jar (3 to 4 oz) _caviar_ into a fine wire strainer and rinse with cool water; let drain.

Combine 2 teaspoons _unflavored gelatin_ and 1/4 cup _dry vermouth_ (or water) in a 1-quart pan; let stand 10 minutes. Stir over medium heat until melted.

In a food processor, combine gelatin, 3 hard-cooked _eggs_, 3/4 cup _sour cream_, ½ cup sliced _green onion_, ¼ cup _parsley_, 3 tablespoons _mayonnaise_, 2 tablespoons _lemon juice_, and 1 teaspoon _prepared horseradish_. Process until egg is finely chopped, (or mash eggs thoroughly with a fork; beat in other ingredients with an electric mixer).

Stir in about 3/4 of the caviar; reserve remainder. Pour into a metal mold (at least 2-cup size, preferably with a flat bottom). Cover and chill until firm, at least 3 hours or until next day.

To serve, dip mold to rim into very hot tap _water_ just until edges begin to liquify. Invert onto a serving dish. Garnish with reserved caviar (more, if you like). Makes 12 to 16 servings.

———

Mr & Mrs Robert Chatham and their guests find this recipe to be a great accompaniment to champagne, and it is served at their Monterey Beach Hotel to VIP guests.

Mr and Mrs Robert Chatham

Gisella Christensen

MAMMA'S DESSERT

"Mama believed in wasting no food"

Two or three day old cake cut in half.
Place in attractive serving dish.
Cover cake with seasonal fruit.
Place other half of cake (or crumbs) on fruit.
Cover with more fruit.
Pour generously at the bottom, rum or sweet sherry.
Let cake absorb liquid for several hours.
Before serving, cover top with whipped cream, or zabaglione sauce.

Zabaglione

6 egg yolks
1 tbsp. water
1 3/4 c. sugar

4/5 qt. Marsala wine
1 c. heavy cream

Combine egg yolks, water, sugar and Marsala wine in top of double boiler. Place over warm water and beat with rotary beater increasing heat of water. Continue beating until mixture is slightly thick and creamy. Remove from over hot water; continue beating until cool. Whip cream until thick; add to mixture. Serve as sauce. Makes about six cups.

Gisella Caccialanza
Mrs Lew Christensen

Ruby Christensen

Holiday Egg-Nog

20 eggs
6 quarts milk
2 pounds powdered sugar
2 quarts cognac or brandy
1½ pints light rum

Separate eggs and add sugar to yolks in large bowl. Beat until well blended, then slowly add brandy. Continue to beat.

Next add rum and milk and when mixture is smooth, refrigerate for an hour or two. Before serving, beat egg whites until fluffy and gently fold into egg-nog. Sprinkle with nutmeg if desired.

When Harold and I moved into our first apartment, we started a tradition of giving modest Xmas Eve parties for all the members of the San Francisco Ballet who were separated from their families during the holidays. Our only request was that each guest bring an inexpensive ornament to hang on our little tree. Through the years, those pretty decorations have brought back many memories of old friends.

We decided that first year, to serve sweets and egg-nog, and coaxed this fine old recipe from the bartender at Al O'Leary's place, which was next door to our ballet school on Van Ness Avenue. The corner café, O'Leary's, and the dance studio are gone now, but a cup of cheer at Xmas time brings it all back to mind.

Sincerely,
Ruby Christensen

SPANISH BUNS

1 lb. sharp cheddar cheese, grated
6 stalks celery, diced to small pieces
1 large green bell pepper, diced to small pieces
1 bunch green onions, sliced thinly (including tops)
1 pint stuffed green olives, sliced
1 cup olive oil
1 can Campbell's tomato soup (undiluted)

Mix together and marinate 24 hours.

Open potato rolls, scoop out center, and fill with cheese
mixture. Bake at 350 degrees 15 or 20 minutes, or until
cheese melts. Serves 20 to 25.

We have served and enjoyed these Spanish Buns many times
as an after theatre light supper. We serve them with a
citrus salad - grapefruit, orange and avocado sections
topped with a sweetpoppy seed dressing.

ENJOY!

William F. Christensen
Artistic Director - Emeritus
San Francisco Ballet

Helgi Tomasson
Artistic Director

Richard E. LeBlond, Jr.
President, Chief Executive Officer

Timothy Duncan
General Manager, Assistant to the President

Evelyn's Enchiladas

1 24 oz can Las Palmas Red Chile Sauce
1 24 oz can Tomato Sauce
1 or 2 bay leaves
Vegetable Oil
2 dozen Corn Tortillas
1 1/2 lbs. sharp cheddar cheese
1 1/2 lbs. Monterey Jack cheese
1 small white onion
1 large tub sour cream (optional)
Cooked chicken or beef may also be added if desired
Chopped olives

In a large pan put enough vegetable oil to cover the bottom. Heat oil til very hot, add red chile sauce, tomato sauce, bay leaves stirring constantly. Simmer for about 45 minutes to one hour stirring occasionally. Into a large bowl grate cheese setting aside 1 cup, mix the rest with finely chopped onion and olives, mix well.

Chile sauce should thicken slightly; if too thick add small amounts of water to thin. Heat a frying pan of oil (enough to cover tortillas) until very hot and begin to fry tortillas on each side until they begin to bubble.

Place on a plate and add chile sauce to to coat tortillas. Place on a cookie sheet and fill with cheese mixture (add chicken or beef if you choose) roll and place in rows. Continue process until desired amount is obtained. There should be enough sauce remaining to spread over the top of the enchilada's. Then sprinkle with cheese, cover with foil, and bake at 350 degrees for about 20 minutes or until cheese is completely melted. Serve hot with sour cream on top. Note: they also freeze well for later meals; handy hint if serving dancers, can be better enjoyed when there is no performance the next day. Serves 6-8

WILLIAM K. COBLENTZ

THIRTY-FIFTH FLOOR
ONE EMBARCADERO CENTER
SAN FRANCISCO, CALIFORNIA 94111

FILLET OF FISH WITH LEEK SAUCE

4 skinless, boneless fillets of
  scrod, about 1-1/4 pounds
  Salt to taste if desired
3 leeks, about 1-1/2 lbs.
9 tablespoons butter
4 tablespoons finely chopped
  shallots
4 teaspoons freshly squeezed
  lemon juice

1/4 cup dry white wine
  Freshly ground pepper
  to taste
1 cup fish broth or bot-
  tled clam juice
1/4 cup finely chopped
  chives or parsley

1. Sprinkle fish on all sides with salt and pepper.

2. Trim off root ends of leeks. Cut each leek crosswise
   in half. Put upper green portion to another use, such
   as soup, or discard.

3. Slice white part of leek lengthwise and rinse thoroughly
   between the leaves. Cut into thin strips, then into very
   thin cubes. There should be about 3-1/2 cups.

4. Heat 2 tablespoons butter in a skillet and add shallots.
   Cook briefly, stirring, and add leeks. Cook, stirring,
   about 2 minutes and add wine and fish broth or clam juice.
   Cover closely and cook 5 minutes. Uncover and cook until
   most of the liquid evaporates. Swirl in 6 tablespoons of
   butter and the chives or parsley.

5. Heat remaining 1 tablespoon of butter in a large, heavy
   skillet and add fish fillets. Cook about 2 minutes on
   one side or until golden brown. Cook about 1 minute
   on second side. Cooking time will depend on thickness
   of fillets. This may have to be done in two batches.

6. Spoon equal batches of the leek mixture into centers
   of four warmed plates. Cover each portion with one
   cooked fillet. Spoon 1 teaspoon of lemon juice over
   each fillet and serve.

Yield: 4 servings.

*This is a simple, healthy entree
for any occasion*

Bill Coblentz

45

San Francisco Chronicle

THE VOICE OF THE WEST

BOB COMMANDAY'S OPERA/BALLET SANDWICH

On returning home after an evening in the Opera House that has involved me fully, I am normally beset by abnormal gnawings of hunger. The more involving the evening, the greater the pangs. I tell myself that I have been participating as fully as the performers and deserve to be indulged. When things haven't gone well in the performance, the craving is more likely to be in the line of thirst, but that's another story.

To meet this midnight crisis without overachieving and putting comfortable rest and a good night's sleep in jeopardy, I improvised the S.O.B. Sandwich (Sweet Old Bob's Sandwich) years ago and have been sleeping on it soundly ever since.

Per serving. (Any number may play)

Take one English muffin or slice of a good rye or black bread, and toast lightly.

Spread with a light layer of cream cheese, and another generous one of sour cream. Dot the surface with thin slices of stuffed green olives and cover with two slices of a small tomato. Grate sharp cheese over this, and dash a bit of Worcestershire sauce on top.

Broil until the cheese is thoroughly melted and the tomato is good and hot and soft.

When you will have then poured a nice white wine or vodka over ice, that will be time enough for this open-face snack to have become cool enough to eat safely.

There are a number of alternative possibilities for the ingredients depending on your ingenuity and what's on hand in the fridge. Caviar if you are out of olives. A touch of grated raw onions or a dash of a good mustard is a nice touch in place of the Worcestershire sauce. Suit yourself. Who deserves it more?

Robert Commanday

(415) 777-1111

SANTA BARBARA WRITER'S CONFERENCE

POST OFFICE BOX 304
CARPINTERIA, CALIFORNIA 93013
(805) 684-2250

THAT ELUSIVE SPANISH SOUP

For years, Mary and I dedicated ourselves to a constant hunt in Spain for a perfect gazpacho recipe -- a simple and common dish which is easy to make -- badly. But we were searching for perfection, and we finally found it in Andalucia. It was in a huge cave in Granada where a 90 year old crone who claimed to have been the prototype for Pilar in <u>For Whom the Bell Tolls</u> made us the ultimate gazpacho, pure pink, glacier-cold ambrosia.

"Give us the recipe!" we implored.

"Obscenity, obscenity, obscenity," she replied, not unkindly.

But we gave her some pesetas and a goatskin full of Kruggerands and she finally relented, as gypsies will.

"Stir it well and true, my little rodents," she intoned, "chill it colder than a Sherpa's nipple, and then when you taste it, the earth will always move for you!"

GAZPACHO

1 slice stale white bread
1 cup water
1 large yellow onion-chopped
1 garlic clove-minced
1 cucumber-peeled, seeded and chopped
1 green Bell pepper-seeded and chopped
6 large tomatoes, skinned and chopped
1 cup tomato juice

Combine all the above with

1/2 cup olive oil
1/2 cup Red Wine Vinegar
Salt to taste

Blenderize and strain into large bowl.
Add 1 tray of ice cubes and refrigerate.

Serve with bowls of

Chopped cucumber
Chopped green Bell peppers
Chopped tomatoes
Small toasted croutons

¡Que se aproveche!
Barnaby Conrad

47

MARION CUNNINGHAM
1147 NORTHGATE ROAD
WALNUT CREEK, CA 94598
(415) 934-3332

Cranberry Raisin Pie (one 9-inch pie)

This pie won first prize in a recipe contest and it deserved to!
Absolutely delicious and very welcome around the holidays with a
cup of homemade eggnog.

Basic pie dough for a two-crust 9-inch pie

2 cups raisins

4 cups fresh cranberries (one cello bag found in supermarkets)

1 cup sugar

1/4 cup Grand Marnier

Zest from 1 large orange, chopped

Preheat the oven to 400F.

Put the raisins, cranberries, sugar, Grand Marnier, and the
orange zest in a large mixing bowl. Toss all the ingredients together until well mixed (using your hands works best).

Roll out half the dough and line the pie pan.

Fill the pan with the cranberry mixture.

Roll out the remaining dough and fit over the filling. Cut
several vents on top.

Bake the pie for 15 minutes, lower the heat to 350F. and continue
to bake for 45 minutes more. Remove from oven and serve warm.

This is the perfect pie for all those who loathe mincemeat pie.

Bert Cutino
P. O. Box 2194
Monterey, California 93940

Being a chef, restaurant owner, and constantly traveling for the American Culinary Federation as Vice President of the Western Region of the United States, I'm constantly tasting and eating foods that are high in calories. So, when I have to diet, and I still need to satisfy my craving for these foods, I prepare my Healthy Pasta dish, which gives me the pleasure of taste and flavors and is most satisfying, without all those calories. It keeps me happy during that time, or any time!

Bert Cutino, Certified Executive Chef
Member of the American Academy of Chefs
Co-owner, Sardine Factory Restaurant,
  Monterey, California

BERT'S HEALTHY PASTA DISH
(Serves 4)

12 oz. Jerusalem Artichoke Fettuccine (Purchase at
  Health Food Store)
2 whole Ripe Tomatoes (deseeded and chopped)
1/2 cup Low Fat Cottage Cheese
1 small Onion (chopped fine)
3 medium Mushrooms (sliced)
1 tsp. Fine Chopped Fresh Garlic
1 Tbsp. Fresh Chopped Basil
1 Tbsp. Fresh Chopped Parsley
1 tsp. Black Pepper
1 tsp. Grated Parmesan Cheese
2 Tbsp. Safflower Oil

Procedure:

Boil pasta for 8 minutes, or until al dente. Then in a large saute pan, add oil and heat. Add onions and mushrooms and simmer. Add tomatoes. Blend well and simmer for one minute. Add basil, garlic, pepper, and parsley. Simmer for another minute. Next, add cottage cheese. Drain pasta and mix in with ingredients in pan. Then put on a serving platter, sprinkle on Parmesan cheese and serve.

Approximate calories per serving: 225

ASSYRIAN RACK OF LAMB   Yield: 4 Portions
                                                 of 3 chops

You will want 1½ lamb racks, each with 8 to 9 ribs.
Ask the butcher to remove the flap of meat and to French
cut the rib bones.

Put into a blender and puree:
                        1 Large Onion
                        2-3 Cloves Garlic
                        1 tsp Basil Leaves
                        ½ tsp Pepper
                        ½ Cup Pomegranate Juice
                        ½ tsp Salt
                        ¼ Cup Red Wine

Rub this marinade well into the racks and put the remaining marinade over the racks in a shallow glass or
enameled pan. Let marinate in refrigerator overnight,
or at cool room temperature for six to eight hours.

Wipe off excess marinade and roast in 450° oven for 15
to 20 minutes for medium rare lamb, longer if you like
lamb done to a greater degree.

Narsai M. David

MRS. RALPH DAVIES
122 LAKEVIEW DRIVE
WOODSIDE, CALIFORNIA 94062

BEST PUMPKIN PIE

This recipe was given to me by a dear kind neighbor long ago. It is delicious! Especially around Thanksgiving time!

1 #2 size can of pumpkin	1/4 tsp. salt
1/4 lb. butter	1 tsp. nutmeg
2 1/2 c. milk	5 eggs, separated
2 tsp. cinnamon (rounded)	$1\frac{1}{2}$ c. sugar

Cream butter with sugar. Add pumpkin, milk, spices, and salt. Add beaten egg yolks; then fold in stiffly beaten egg whites. Bake in rich unbaked pie crust at 350 degrees for 45 minutes or until knife inserted at side comes out clean.

Makes two pies.

Happy Eating!

CREAM OF CORN SOUP
(serves 12)

Rub 6 cans cream style corn through a sieve. Add 1 quart milk and 1 pint half and half. Mix 1 teaspoon curry powder (more if needed after tasting) in a little of the milk and add with salt and pepper to taste. Heat about 45 minutes over very low heat, and stir constantly.

Sally Debenham

DeBolt Productions

Post Office Box 11211
Oakland, California 94611
(415) 547-4190 or 658-8458

FAVORITE RECIPE FROM DOROTHY AND ROBERT DeBOLT

BLACK BEAN SOUP

Rinse 1 pound (2 cups) black beans in cold water, picking them over well. Put them in a large pot with 1 coarsely chopped large yellow onion, 2 cups chopped plum tomatoes, 6 large peeled garlic cloves, 3 bay leaves, ½ teaspoon whole thyme and 1 tablespoon coarsely ground black pepper. (We add extra garlic and pepper to suit our taste.)

Cover with 4 to 6 cups chicken stock, and add a ham bone or ham hock. Bring to a boil, reduce the heat and simmer slowly, uncovered, adding more stock or water as needed and stirring from the bottom frequently, until the beans are very soft and have thickened the soup.

Season with salt to taste. Serve garnished with finely chopped white onion and fresh cilantro.

We prefer the beans whole, but they can be pureed if desired. This soup is wonderful, and tastes even better the second day!

This recipe is also a great favorite of all twenty of our children, but when they were home it was in "mega quantities"!

Dorothy De Bolt   Robert W DeBolt

53

Now Presenting
Together for the First Time
STRANGE DE JIM
P.O. Box 14547
San Francisco, CA 94114

CHICO DELIGHT

One box Ritz crackers
One pound Velveeta cheese
One pint finest caviar

Rip open the box of crackers. Lavishly spread on the Velveeta. Pile on the caviar. This dish can frankly appall any number of guests and earn you an instant reputation as a Julia Child molester. Bon appetit!

Strange de Jim

Keep An Eye On The Bluebird ...

The San Francisco Ballet Association Auxiliary is putting out a cookbook and asked me to submit a recipe. I thought I'd give them this one from the pool hall in Tepic:

YOU NEED A JIGGER of tequila. This is just to sip. It's not part of the mix. You sip the tequila and follow it with sangrita. It will grow hair on you.

Sangrita: *One cup of orange juice. One quarter cup of lemon juice. One eighth cup of grenadine syrup. One small onion chopped fine. Three large drops of Tabasco — the Mexican hot sauce. This can be varied according to how hot you like it. It's a firecracker, so be careful.*

Let it stand overnight. Then put the juice through a strainer to get rid of the onions. Put in a pinch of salt.

Pour a jigger of tequila. Another jigger of the sangrita.

Don't mix them. A sip of one. A sip of the other. Salud!

Hope these spice up your cookbook.

Benedictions,

Stan Delaplane

SD

Stan Delaplane . . . . **San Francisco Chronicle**

GEORGE DEUKMEJIAN
GOVERNOR

GOLD COAST SHRIMP

2	pounds medium to large shrimp, cooked and deveined
6	oranges, peeled, sliced and quartered
4	onions, peeled, cut in half and sliced
1/4	cup sugar
4	teaspoons salt
1	teaspoon Lawry's Seasoned Pepper
2	teaspoons mustard seed
1	teaspoon celery seed
1/2	teaspoon crushed red pepper
2	tablespoons sweet pepper flakes
2	tablespoons minced parsley
1	clove garlic, crushed
1½	cups cider vinegar
1	cup salad oil
2/3	cup fresh lemon juice
1/2	cup ketchup

Place shrimp, oranges and onions in bowl.
Combine remaining ingredients and pour over
shrimp mixture. Cover and marinate in the
refrigerator one to two days; stirring morning
and evening. Drain well. Serve as a first
course in sea shells or in avocado halves. Makes
12 to 16 servings.

* * * *

ARMENIAN SALAD

Mix together in a salad bowl:

4	cups tomatoes
2/3	to 1 cup green pepper
1/2	cup parsley
1/2	cup scallions
2	sliced cucumbers
1/4	cup lemon juice
2	teaspoons salt

Mix together, toss and serve immediately. Serves
6.

George Deukmejian

Mrs. George Deukmejian

November 20, 1986

TO THE SAN FRANCISCO BALLET:

I wish the San Francisco Ballet all my best
in the coming season. I hope you enjoy my recipe
for Flank Steak.

Best wishes,

Gloria Deukmejian

Gloria Deukmejian

Flank Steak

1	cup soy sauce
1	cup California Sherry
1/3	cup peanut oil
2	small cloves garlic, minced
1/3	cup chopped or grated fresh ginger or
1/2	teaspoon ground ginger
2	Flank Steaks

Blend soy, sherry, oil, garlic and ginger. Marinate
the Flank Steaks in the mixture for several hours,
turning occasionally. Grill over brisk coals three
to four minutes per side for rare, five minutes
per side for medium.

PARFAIT AU CAFE

2 cups sugar
1½ cups double-strength coffee
½ teaspoon salt
6 large egg white
3 teaspoons vanilla extract
5 cups heavy cream, (4 for mixture, 1 for topping)
Kahlua liqueur
chocolate sprinkles

Combine sugar and in small saucepan. Bring to boiling,
stirring constantly. Boil rapidly, without stirring,
about 5 minutes, or until candy thermometer reads 234, or
until syrup forms a soft small ball when dropped into cold
water. Remove syrup from heat and cool about 1 minute.
Meanwhile, add the salt to the egg whites and beat until
they stand up in soft, stiff peaks. Pour the hot syrup
in a fine stream over the beaten egg whites, beating the
mixture all the while. Add the vanilla extract, and
continue beating until whipped cream. Turn the mixture
into champagne or parfait glasses. Cover with foil.
Freeze without stirring until the mixture is firm.
Remove from freezer after soup or main course. Add
whipped cream topping and chocolate sprinkles, and serve.
Serves 6 to 8 people.

Margot de Wildt

Herb fettucine with butter, cheese and garlic sauce

INGREDIENTS
1/2 pound butter, at room temperature
6 cloves garlic, finely minced
1 teaspoon salt
3/4 cup freshly grated combination Parmesan/Romano cheese
1/4 cup fresh basil
Black pepper to taste
One pound herb fettucine

1) Cream together the butter, garlic and salt until mixture is smooth. Put in bottom of large serving dish.

2) When the pasta is cooked al dente (90 seconds in boiling water), drain, put in serving dish with sauce and toss well. Add Parmesan cheese and basil and toss again.

3) Serve in individual dishes and sprinkle pepper on top. Shallow soup bowls work best because they keep the butter, which melts upon contact with the hot pasta, from running off to the side.

As often happens with the dishes I cook, I've made changes in the basic recipe. For instance: I put in twice as much garlic, because I believe twice as much garlic is four times as good; I combine Parmesan and Romano (instead of straight Parmesan) for a slightly sharper taste; I added basil, to give the dish pungency; and I use herb fettucine because I think it works better than spaghettini.

A light Italian red, such as Dolcetto d'Alba, Merlot or Chianti (Isole e Olena is my current favorite) is especially delicious with this. Both the wine and the food glide down the throat.

*   *   *

This is one of the simplest dishes I cook and, because of its high fat content, one in which I indulge only occasionally. But my 16-year-old son, Scott, the true gourmet in the family (he has an autographed menu from Paul Bocuse) tells me it's my best, and the reaction I get from dinner guests confirms that.

Once, we hosted sports attorney Leigh Steinberg and his wife, Lucy, and former Stanford and 49er quarterback Guy Benjamin and his fiancee, Jill Barnes, to celebrate the engagement of Guy and Jill. Jill said, "This is the best pasta I've ever had." At the conclusion of the meal, which included gazpacho, sauteed veal with prosciutto, gruyere and Marsala wine and home-made (by Scott) raspberry ice cream, Jill told me, "I want you to cater our wedding dinner."

Glenn Dickey
Chronicle sports columnist

ELEANOR DICKINSON

Mrs. Benziger's Fruit Cake Recipe

cream, beat or mix in order

½ lb margarine
2 cups brown sugar
5 eggs
2 to 4 cups flour (test)
small jars of tart jelly
and marmalade
1 Tsp cinnamon, ½ tsp cloves
1 tsp. salt, ½ tsp. allspice
1 tsp. nutmeg
1 tsp. soda dissolved in
juice of ½ lemon ~
1 lb. cherries
1 lb. white raisins
½ lb. pineapple
½ lb citron
1 lb. nuts

ELEANOR DICKINSON

Flour the fruit ~ fold in
Test small sample
to determine flour ~
Grease pans, line them,
fill ½ full ~

~ Decorate tops ~

bake slowly 1¼ hours
or until firm ~
cool in pan ~
enjoy ~

—Eleanor Dickinson
P.S. I always triple the
recipe so I can give
cakes to family and friends

Genevieve Di San Faustino —
HOT CAULIFLOWER SALAD

(cauliflower, olive oil, garlic, mustard, vinegar.)

① Trim a white cauliflower & scald it in cold water for ½ hour. Divide it into flowerettes. Reassemble them in the semblance of a whole cauliflower.

② Heat 6 T of olive oil; + in it, steep 1 minced garlic clove over low heat. Stir in; ½ t. mustard, 2 T wine vinegar, salt & pepper plus 1 t. minced parsley. Blend the dressing well + pour it over the cauliflower.

③ Reassemble the whole mixture + place in a gratin dish + serve.

This can be served cold in which case do not heat the dressing. Simple.-!
Serves four.

Tiffany & Co.

252 Grant Avenue
San Francisco, CA 94108

415-781-7000

Charles Dishman

Divisional Vice President

Breakfast on Tiffany's:

　　Enjoy breakfast on Tiffany's with Tiffany's Monet pattern of china. A beautiful blue and yellow china reminiscent of Monet's home at Giverny. Your orange juice and champagne will be served in Baccarat's Prelude champagne flute, and your sparkling mineral water from the Prelude water goblet. The breakfast will start with fresh berries with coconut cream served in a simple, yet elegant Baccarat salad dish followed by scrambled eggs with lamb and rosemary sausage. Also served with the eggs, is a sweet potato pancake with cinnamon sour cream. Finally, the skillet cornbread with fresh plum jam will be presented on a lovely white weave tray only available at Tiffany's.

　　Isn't this a wonderful way to start the day?

MAGAZINE

LANE PUBLISHING CO.

Being very fond of Burgundy, where we repeatedly relish the pleasures of canal traveling, we have come to treasure the lovely Creme de Cassis of this region and always bring a bottle or two home. The cordial, well made, is the very essence of black currants. Paired with raspberries, slightly heated to bring out their sunshine flavor, Creme de Cassis gives the fruit a sensual, briery intensity. Served with gelato, and perhaps a puff of whipped cream, the effect is showstopping, and wonderfully simple.

SUN-WARM RASPBERRIES WITH CASSIS

4 cups fresh raspberries
1 or 2 tablespoons sugar
About ½ cup Creme de Cassis
1 pint vanilla-bean gelato
½ cup whipping cream, whipped to hold soft peaks

Sort berries carefully, discarding any that are decayed. Reserving the most perfectly shaped berries, measure 1½ cups raspberries and place in a 1- to 2-quart pan. Add sugar to taste and 3 tablespoons of the Creme de Cassis to fruit in the pan. Place over medium-high heat and stir gently until berries begin to break apart and liquid is boiling. Add the reserved berries and mix very gently, then remove from heat at once.

Quickly, scoop the gelato equally into 4 dessert bowls or rimmed plates. Surround each serving with the warm berries. Offer the remaining Creme de Cassis and the whipped cream to add to taste to each serving. Or you can pour a little of the Creme de Cassis over the ice cream to give it a splash of color, then present with the optional toppings. Makes 4 servings.

Food & Wine Editor
SUNSET Magazine

Dagmar Dolby

CHOCOLATE BRANDY CAKE

This used to be a favorite with guests on our boat during
a Sunday picnic on the Thames or the Bay. It is easy to
make and to transport. The rum goes with the boating spirit.
There is only one hitch -- very rich and not possible on a
low cholestrol diet!
But for the sake of good memories, here it is...

2 1/2 c Graham cracker crumbs
1/2 lb semi-sweet chocolate
1/2 butter (try margarine!)
2 eggs
3/4 c sugar
2 oz chopped dried apricots
2 oz walnut halves
Brandy or rum

Melt chocolate and butter over low heat; beat eggs and sugar together;
add to chocolate mixture; mix in fruit, nuts, and brandy. Put in mold
or loaf tin; decorate with some of the nuts and fruit. Store in refrigerator
until 1/2 hour before serving.

Dagmar Dolby

A.C.T.
AMERICAN CONSERVATORY THEATRE

FILLET OF SOLE MOUSSE WITH SHRIMP SAUCE

We serve this lovely, delicate mousse with our favorite Chardonnay wine on festive occasions.

THE MOUSSE

1 lb. fillet of sole
2 cups whipping cream
4 extra large eggs
2/3 cup milk
1 Tbsp. parsley flakes*
1 1/2 tsp. salt
1/4 tsp. savory
1/8 tsp. white pepper
cayenne
1 Tbsp. butter
2 Tbsp. dry bread crumbs
1/2 tsp. dill weed

Cut 1 lb. fillet of sole in small pieces. Place about 1/2 cup of heavy cream in the food processor, add 1/4 of the fish and process until smooth. Add 1 whole egg, scrape down with rubber spatula, and process again until smooth. Mixture will become very thick. Turn out into a bowl and repeat until all of the fish is blended with the remaining cream and eggs. Stir in the milk, parsley, salt, savory, white pepper, and a dash of cayenne. Mix well. Spread 1 Tbsp. butter in a 6 cup ring mold. Combine the bread crumbs with the dill weed and sprinkle over the bottom and sides of the mold. Spoon the mixture into the mold and level top with a spatula. Set in a pan of hot water.

Bake in a 350° oven for 45 minutes. Top will be lightly browned and a knife inserted in the center will come out clean. Let stand 15 minutes. Remove from mold. Serve with shrimp sauce. Makes 6 servings.

SHRIMP SAUCE

2 cups shrimp
1/4 cup butter
3 Tbsp. flour
1 1/2 cups cream
   (Half and Half)
1/2 tsp salt
1/2 tsp. onion powder
3 Tbsp. dry sherry
1 Tbsp. lemon juice
2 tsp. parsley flakes*

Melt 1/4 cup butter and stir in the flour. Add the Half and Half cream, salt and onion powder. Cook until the sauce boils and thickens. Stir in sherry, lemon juice and parsley. Add the shrimp and heat through. Makes 3 cups of sauce.

*I recommend fresh parsley, finely chopped, if available.

FEAST AND ENJOY!

PETER DONAT

450 Geary Street, San Francisco, California 94102 (415) 771-3880
A Non-Profit Tax Exempt Foundation

JEROME C. DRAPER, JR.

75 BROADWAY, SUITE 207
SAN FRANCISCO, CALIFORNIA 94111
(415) 398-8898

TELEX 470517 WIL UI

FRESH OYSTER DOLMADES

Water	- 3 quarts
Salt	- 1 TB
Large, flat spinach leaves	- 30
Large oysters	- 24
Clam juice	- 1/2 cup
Salt	- to taste
Freshly ground white pepper	- to taste
Freshly ground nutmeg	- to taste
Unsalted butter	- 2 TB
Fresh lemon juice	- 3 TB
Black caviar	- 1 TB
Pimiento	- 2 tsp
Lemon	- 1

Trim the spinach leaves, dice the pimiento finely and slice the lemon thinly.
Bring the water and the salt to a boil in a 4-quart saucepan.
Add the spinach and cook for 30 seconds.
Drain and carefully transfer the leaves to a bowl of ice water. Do not
  tear.
Combine the oysters with their liquor and the clam juice, in a small saucepan.
Simmer the oysters until barely cooked over a high heat.
Drain well.
Spread the spinach leaves on a towel.
Place an oyster off center toward the top of each leaf.
Season each lightly with salt, pepper and nutmeg.
Wrap each oyster by folding the tip of the leaf over first, and then the two
  opposite sides. Roll each oyster toward the stem end of the leaf to make
  neat packages.
Melt the butter in a large skillet over medium heat.
Arrange the dolmades seam side down, and reheat for 3 minutes until just barely
  warm.
Transfer to a serving dish.
Add the lemon juice to the skillet and heat through.
Pour into a small bowl and stir in the caviar.
Spoon sparingly over the dolmades.
Dot each dolmades with 1 or 2 pieces of pimiento and garnish the dish with the
  lemon slices.
Serves 8.

Marvelous with Champagne as a first course. Even those who don't eat oysters
relish this dish.

Jerome C. Draper, Jr.

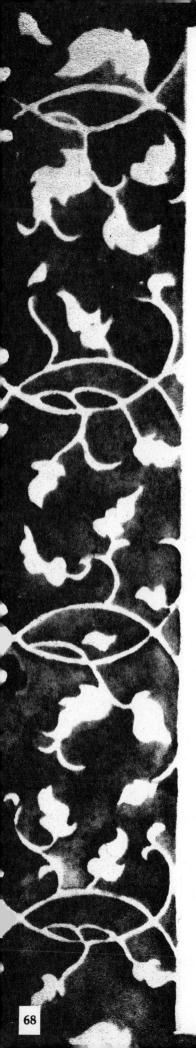

Clarissa Dyer

A HUNTER'S DELIGHT

(Different, Easy, Delicious. Given to me by a
Friend in France)

TINY QUAIL IN POTATO BASKETS

4 Quail
4 Baking Potatoes
9 tbs Butter
2 tbs Coriander
Salt, Pepper to taste

METHOD

I.   Preheat oven to 450 degrees. Bake potatoes,
     washed but not peeled, 1 hour.

II. Grill coriander in frying pan. Shake to grill grains
     evenly. Spread on towel and grind to fine powder with
     rolling pin. Shake through sieve onto plate. Put aside.

III. 15 minutes before potatoes are done, salt and pepper
     quail inside and out. In heavy pan, add half the
     butter and brown quail on all sides. Cover and cook
     for 15 minutes. Keep warm.

IV. When potatoes are baked, remove from oven. Cut off
     top slice, lengthwise, about ½ inch thick. Put slices
     aside. Scoop out inside without damaging skins and
     put into bowl (don't let it get cold). Mix in
     remaining butter with coriander. Salt and pepper to
     taste, and mash until smooth. Spoon pulp to 1/3
     capacity of each potato skin. Place quail, prepared as
     above, in each potato skin and push down. Cover with
     rest of mashed potato and smooth. Top with cut-off
     slices. Return to oven for 5 minutes.

V.   Serve on bed of lettuce (raddicio or whatever is in
     season). Also, fresh vegetable and parsley to
     garnish.

     Serve with nice Bordeaux.

Clarissa Dyer

GARLIC MINT SALAD DRESSING

1 clove garlic
2 Tblsp. lime juice
1 tsp. Dijon mustard
½ tsp. dried mint

1/8 tsp. sugar
1/4 tsp. salt
1/3 cup vegetable oil

Place all ingredients in blender except oil. Add
oil a drop at a time while blending til smooth.

Clint Eastwood

PASTA FAGIOLI

INGREDIENTS

2 Tbs. Olive Oil

5 cloves garlic

1 large onion

1 28 oz. can peeled tomatoes

1 15 oz can tomato puree

1 6 oz. can tomato paste

1 15 oz. can white kidney beans

1 tbs. oregano

1 tbs. basil

1 bay leaf

a squeeze of fresh lemon juice

1 tbs. sugar

salt

pepper

20 oz. macaroni or
   other pasta

PROCEDURE

Saute the onion and minced garlic in the olive oil. You can chop or slice the onion, whichever you prefer. Boil the pasta al dente. Add all the rest of the ingredients! Try whole wheat pasta. It's better for you, and the taste isn't much different in a recepie like this. Use fresh tomatoes for a less salty version.This meal is nutritious, cheap and very low in calories. It's my favorite.

Dr. Dean Edell

1500 Sutter Street at Gough, San Francisco 94109, 415 776-6400

Nov. 7, 1986

The recipe for Pumpkin and Red Pepper Slippers was conceived by me and my co-chefs, Peter De Marais and John Struer, at the Cafe Majestic just after the pumpkin season started. As we always do, we were looking for a novel way to use fresh, seasonal ingredients. The stuffed slippers therefore came into being, not without a certain whimsy. How fortuitous, then, that the recipe had just been invented when I was asked to contribute to the San Francisco Ballet cookbook. What better dish could be offered to a dance company?

Pumpkin and Red Pepper Slippers

3 cups pumpkin meat
3 shallots, minced
3 cloves garlic, minced
½ cup grated parmesan cheese
1 cup brown sugar
½ cup heavy cream
pinch of cayenne
salt to taste

4 small to medium red bell peppers

1-2 tablespoons butter
½ teaspoon minced fresh ginger

Instructions: Mix together in blender pumpkin, seasoning and cream. Add cream sparingly so that mixture is not too loose.

Prepare red peppers by lying them on side and slicing off a top section to give them the shape of a slipper. Retain the portion that's removed. Seed the peppers. Spoon or pipe in pumpkin mixture. Cover with sliced-off section.
Place in baking pan. Bake 15 minutes in hot oven (450-475°). Put on hot plate. Then make a simple butter sauce by sauteing butter and ginger until sizzling. Pour over peppers. Use sprig of watercress as garnish. Serve as appetizer, or lunch entree. 4 servings.

Stanley Eichelbaum

elina's closet at ı. magnin

HIMAM BAYELDI

8 eggplants (medium size)
3 large onions, 3 large tomatoes
1 bunch chopped parsley, ½ cup pine nuts
½ cup currants, salt, pepper, dash of sugar

Cut off about one inch from the top of the eggplants and fry
each eggplant on all sides in some olive oil until very slightly
tender. Carefully quarter each eggplant lengthwise without going
through the bottom, trying to keep them intact.

In a small amount of olive oil, saute gently the minced onions.
Add the rest of the ingredients (the tomatoes cleaned of their
skin and in small pieces). Saute another few minutes, mixing well.

Stuff the opening of each eggplant with the mixture, pressing gently
so the eggplant will not break or separate. You can also keep them
together by using some string.

Place them upright close to each other in a pan. Add 1 cup of hot water.
Cover tightly and bake in a medium heat oven for about one hour, or until
the water is cooked away. Watch the cooking.

Take off the top, let it cool. Arrange the eggplant in the serving plate.
Decorate with black olives, slices of lemon and small bouquets of parsley.

The taste enhances if made a day in advance. It is to be served cold.
It is very colorful.

The legend says when the Shah tasted it, he fainted of ecstasy.

*Best wishes to
The San Francisco Ballet*

The Butcher
est. 1977
merle ellis

POST OFFICE BOX 907
TIBURON, CALIFORNIA 94920
(415) 383-6585

A Yorkshire specialty served in London during the Holiday season is a kind of poultry pie, a turkey or a goose or some similarly festive bird, boned and stuffed with another, boned and stuffed with another, etc., etc. And then all wrapped and baked in a thick pastry shell so it could be carried "over the river and through the woods to grandmother's house . . ."

I've never carried one quite like that, but I have borrowed the idea and simplified it a bit to make a festive and memorable meal for any season, made from an inexpensive chicken stuffed with another inexpensive chicken stuffed with another . . . It makes a great meal guaranteed to bring oohs and aahs from your assembled guests —and it's really easy to prepare.

First, place the bird on your cutting board, breast down, and, with the point of your knife, make a slit along the backbone from the neck to the tail. Now lift the skin around the neck to the tail. Now lift the skin around the neck with one hand and, using just the point of the knife, and making small cuts, free the meat from the backbone. Cut as close to the bone as you can and take your time. Try not to cut through the skin. When you reach the thigh joints, cut through them carefully and proceed on.

Once the entire backbone has been loosened and is free of the leg and wing joints, it simplifies the process to remove it. Cut through the cartilage between the ribs and the breast on both sides and lift the backbone out. With the backbone gone, the rest is just like boning out the breast. Remove the keel bone, find the little handles and lift out both sides of the rib cage cutting through the joint where the wing is attached. Leave the wing on the bird. Then remove the wishbone.

Finally, carefully cut through the joint between the leg and the thigh and remove the thigh bone. DO NOT cut through the skin underneath. Leave the drumstick and the wing intact. SAVE ALL THE BONES for the stockpot.

What you now have is a slab of boneless chicken with the legs and wings attached. You're well over half-way home. To complete the job, you will also need one boneless, skinless chicken breast, flattened slightly, one hard-cooked egg and one recipe of your favorite stuffing.

Lay the boned chicken on the cutting board skin side down. Spread a layer of stuffing on top of the meat, place the boneless chicken breast on top of the stuffing and spread a layer of stuffing on top of that. Place a peeled hard-cooked egg right in the middle of the stuffing. Bring the two sides of the chicken together, fasten them at one-inch intervals with toothpicks or metal skewers, then lace up with string. Turn the whole thing over and mold it back into something resembling the original bird.

After your boneless bird is roasted and the skewers and strings are removed, it is ready to be presented and rather simply carved —much to the surprise of assembled guests.

To carve: Place the bird before the carver just as you would a more conventional model. First remove the wings, then slice the bird crosswise into ½-inch thick slices. Each will be a pinwheel of meat, dressing, meat, dressing — and in the middle, an egg. Beautiful!

From "Cutting-up in the Kitchen" by Merle Ellis
Illustrations by Kay Solomon
(Chronicle Books $5.95)

Oakland Ballet

A CALIFORNIA DANCE COMPANY

VEAL LOMBARDI

(for two)

3/4 lb. veal scallopini, thinly sliced
1/4 cup (apx.) grated Parmesan cheese
1/8-1/4 cup butter
  2 shallots, finely chopped
1/2-3/4 cup thinly sliced mushrooms
1/4 teaspoon salt
1/2 chicken bouillon cube
1/4 cup dry Marsala wine

Dip veal in Parmesan cheese. Melt butter in large frying pan.
Cook meat until lightly browned. Remove from pan and place on
platter in very low oven. Cook mushrooms and shallots in pan
with additional butter, if necessary. Add salt, crushed
bouillon cube and Marsala wine. Cook for a few minutes until
mushrooms soften. Return veal to pan and stir for one minute.
Serve on a heated platter, pouring sauce and mushrooms over
veal. Serve with rice.

Veal Lombardi is a dish I served while living in Italy.
The fresh ingredients are essential as is the spirit of
Italy in enjoying this dish. It provided many a warm
and romantic evening as the sun turned golden on the
vine-covered hills of Carrara, Italy.

Enjoy,
Betsy Erickson

CULINARY COMPANY

Cooking School, Cookware, Delicatessen and The Party Solution

QUICHES

Tender crispy pastry shells filled with rich custard are always a cocktail favorite. They can be baked in rectangular tart molds, (for easy service) or in 2 or 3" individual tart molds. There is no limit to the variety of fillings that may be added to the basic custard; Roquefort cheese, smoked salmon, ham, cheese, crab, shrimp, mushrooms, clams, sweet peppers, spinach, zucchini, tomatoes and so on.

JE-H ZUCCHINI QUICHE   20 Servings/Or about 15 miniatures·
Ingredients

JE-H basic plain pastry 2 medium zucchini
2 oz Parmesan Reggiano 4 oz Swiss Gruyere cheese
3 large eggs 1 1/2 cups Creme Fraiche
freshly grated nutmeg salt/freshly ground white pepper
11"x8" fluted tart mold, removable bottom/15 2" tart molds
Method
1. Roll out the pastry and line the mold.
2. Grate the Parmesan, Gruyere and zucchini finely.Sprinkle over pastry.
5. Combine the eggs, cream, nutmeg, salt and pepper. Pour the custard over the zucchini.
6. Adjust the oven rack to the lowest position, cover with an unglazed stoneware tile and preheat oven to 450F for 20 minutes.
7. Bake the tart in it's mold directly on the tile for 10 minutes. Lower the oven to 375F and bake approximately 25 minutes more, until set.
8. Allow tart to rest at least 30 minutes before cutting.

JE-H BASIC PLAIN PASTRY
Ingredients
10 oz flour (1 1/2 cups) 1/2 tsp. salt
1/2 tsp. vinegar 5 oz. unsalted butter
up to 4 oz ice water
Method
1. Combine the flour, salt and butter until mixture is crumbly.
2. Add the water slowly until the dough gathers together.
3. Wrap in plastic, and allow the dough to rest in a cool place at least 1 hour before rolling out.

THE FAY IMPROVEMENT COMPANY
FINANCIAL CONSULTING AND BUSINESS VENTURES
P.O. BOX 2831
SAN FRANCISCO, CALIFORNIA 94126-2831

PAUL B. FAY, JR.
PRESIDENT

ONLY FOR THE DEMANDING BARBECUED HAMBURGER CONNOISSEUR

Very Important Conditions

1) Only serve when we are on daylight savings time, and then between the hours of 7 - 8 P.M.

2) Limit the group to be served to no more than six, otherwise you will lose control.

3) Have the wife or housekeeper fire up the briquettes 30 minutes before you plan to start cooking. A Weber pot barbecue pit is recommended because it controls the heat distribution.

4) The afternoon of your presentation have the wife or housekeeper go to the market and purchase the following for 6 servings:

   3 lbs. of top ground round
   1½ lbs. of ground chuck
   1 package of eight hamburger buns with sesame seeds
   1 large white onion
   ½ lb. of butter

5) An hour before cooking have the wife or housekeeper cut the onion into small pieces and shred two of the eight buns.

6) Have the wife or housekeeper fry the shredded buns in butter till brown.

7) Have the wife or housekeeper mix all ingredients together evenly and shape into patties between an 1¼ - 1½ inches thick.

8) Mix and serve all the guests, including the wife, a dry martini in a chilled wine glass with a lemon twist (one or two pieces of ice is optional).

9) Uncork two bottles of Jordan 82 or 83 Cabernet Sauvignon.

10) Ten minutes before serving, order the wife or housekeeper to put on the patties, toast on one side for two minutes, then flip over and cook for six more minutes with the top of the Weber barbecue on with holes open.

11) After a total of eight minutes instruct the wife or housekeeper to remove the Weber top, and push the patties to the side for one minute while toasting the buns.

12) Then have the wife or housekeeper serve preferably with fresh picked that day Webb Ranch corn cooked for ten minutes.

Pridefully

Paul B. "Red" Fay, Jr.

Office of the Mayor
San Francisco

DIANNE FEINSTEIN

Chicken Breasts in Parmesan Cream

6 split chicken breasts (3 whole)
    skinned and boned
5 stalks celery, chopped
3 medium (4 small) tomatoes, chopped
1 tsp. tarragon, salt and pepper to taste
2/3 cup parmesan (fresh grated)
2 cups heavy cream
dash of paprika

Place the chicken in large baking pan and sprinkle with half the cheese. Surround chicken with celery and tomato and sprinkle with seasonings. Pour the cream over and sprinkle with the rest of the cheese.

Bake in preheated 350 degree oven for about 50 minutes.

UPSIDE-DOWN PEAR TART WITH RUM AND WALNUTS

This pear tart resembles the familar apple tart, tart tatin. It is made upside-down and then unmolded before serving.

Crust (Pate Sucrée):

2 cups all-purpose flour, cold, sifted
1 1/2 sticks sweet butter, cold, hard, and cut in small cubes
1/3 cup sugar
2 eggs, beaten with a fork
Optional: 1/2 cup finely ground walnuts or pecans, filberts, almonds

Combine dry ingredients, including ground nuts if desired. Cut or work in butter until even and size of peas. Add part of beaten egg and work in lightly with fingers. Continue adding egg until pastry can be formed into ball. (You may need half to all of the egg depending upon the moisture in your flour.) Wrap pastry ball and let rest in refrigerator at least one hour.

8 to 10 hard pears, peeled, halved, stems and core removed -- enough to cover the bottom of a 10" X 14" glass baking pan. Bosc or Comice are good varieties.
3/4 cup sugar
1/4 cup Myer's Dark Rum ← *The best!*
1 cup select walnut halves

Put pears in one layer, rounded side down, in a large (10" X 14") glass baking pan. Sprinkle with all of the sugar. Sprinkle with most of the rum. Bake pears in a 375° oven 45 minutes to an hour until evenly brown and caramelized. Allow to cool, then use these pears in the tart below. *You want a dark amber color!*

Place walnut halves in bottom of a 9-inch glass pie pan. Place baked pear halves, rounded side down, in pie pan. Include any pear syrup you can salvage from baking pan. Sprinkle with balance of the rum. Roll out pastry dough and cover pie. (Make cinnamon-sugar cookies from left-over dough.) Cut edges even with outside edge of pie pan. Roll outside edge of dough inward to form a thick rim on the crust. Push this thick rim inside and down against the pears. This helps support the pie when unmolded. Pierce dough several times with a knife to allow steam to escape. Bake at 350° for 30 to 45 minutes or until crust is nicely browned and done. Let cool at least 30 minutes before unmolding. Place serving dish over pie crust and unmold the upside-down pear tart. Brush top of tart with any excess syrup. Serve slightly warm with vanilla ice cream.

Irresistible!

Tom Ferrell
President

• • •

PANE DI FICHI / FIG BREAD

The first thing to be said about this bread is that it is succulent and delicious as well as very easy to make. The second thing to be noted is that a bread like this has a lot of history behind it. This bread undoubtedly dates back at least to the early Middle Ages, a time when cities like Perugia, Florence, and Siena were dotted with tower houses that gave warring families and factions a good view of their neighbors and enemies. Even though bakers were busy making the daily bread, they made a point of transforming the dough for Sundays and special celebrations by sweetening it with honey and enriching it with nuts or dried fruits, such as figs.

Makes 1 round loaf

2 1/2 teaspoons (1 package) active dry yeast or 1 small cake
  (18 grams) fresh yeast
1 cup warm water
1 1/2 tablespoons olive oil
About 3 cups (375 grams) unbleached all-purpose flour, plus 2
  tablespoons for the figs
1 teaspoon (5 grams) salt
1 cup (200 grams) figs, preferably Calimyrna or Greek string
  figs, cut into about 12 pieces each

Stir the yeast into the water in a large mixing bowl; let stand until creamy, about 10 minutes. Stir in the oil. Mix 3 cups flour and the salt and stir into the yeast mixture. Stir until the dough comes together. Knead on a floured surface, sprinkling with additional flour, until velvety and moist, 7 to 10 minutes.

First Rise. Place the dough in a lightly oiled bowl, cover tightly with plastic wrap, and let rise until doubled, about 1 hour.

Filling. Toss the figs in 2 tablespoons flour to coat the surfaces. Turn the dough out onto a floured surface. Without punching it down, pat the dough into an oval and spread half the figs evenly over the surface; roll up the dough. Pat the dough into an oval again and sprinkle evenly with the remaining figs; roll it up again. Shape into a round loaf, being gentle but, at the same time, pulling the skin taut over the figs. Place the loaf, rough side down, on a lightly floured peel or oiled baking sheet, cover with a towel, and let rise until doubled, 1 1/4 to 1 1/2 hours.

Baking. Thirty minutes before baking, heat the oven with a baking stone in it to 450 degrees F. Sprinkle the stone with cornmeal just before sliding the loaf onto it. Bake 15 minutes. Reduce the heat to 375 degrees F. and bake 15 minutes longer. Cool completely on a rack.

Carol Field

CHOCOLATE CREAM SILK

Chocolate Cake

1 cup all purpose flour
3/4 cup white sugar
3/4 cup brown sugar
1/4 cup cocoa
1/2 cup boiling water
1/2 cup butter
1 cup buttermilk
1 1/2 tsp baking soda
1 tsp salt
1 tsp vanilla
2 beaten eggs

Preheat oven to 350 f / 180 c / Gas 4

Grease and flour an 8 or 9 inch deep spring form pan.

Cream the two sugars with the butter. Blend cocoa with
enough boiling water to form a smooth paste. Add eggs,
vanilla and cocoa mixture to butter and sugar; blend well.
Fold in sifted flour, salt and baking soda alternately with
the buttermilk. Pour into prepared pan. Bake 25 - 30
minutes or until a knife comes out clean when inserted into
the middle of the cake.

Remove the sides of the spring form pan, but leave the cake
sitting on its base. When cold, cut cake in half. Replace
the sides of the pan leaving the bottom half of the cake
sitting on the base.

Cream Silk

1/4 cup sugar
1 egg
14 oz. cream cheese
4 1/2 tsp gelatin
4 tsp water
3 tbsp vanilla
1/2 pint whipping cream
1 lb. white chocolate

Mrs. Fields Cookies
333 Main Street
P.O. Box 4000, Park City, Utah 84060-4000
(801) 649-1304 • Fax (801) 649-1403 • Telex: 494-5743

Decoration

4 cups chopped macadamia nuts/or flaked almonds
1/4 pint whipping cream
1 oz. dark chocolate
confectioners sugar
cocoa powder

Beat cream cheese, egg and sugar until smooth. Melt
chocolate in a double boiler. Sprinkle gelatin into the
water; dissolve over a pan of hot water. Beat into cheese
cake mixture. Add cream to mixture, beat until it thickens.
Fold in chocolate.

Pour mixture into cake pan; carefully place second half of
cake on top. Refrigerate for several hours, when firm
remove pan sides.

Coat sides of cake with chopped macadamia nuts, dust top
with sugar and cocoa. Decorate with rosettes of cream,
chocolate shavings and chopped macadamia nuts.

Sports Illustrated

———

TIME & LIFE BUILDING
NEW YORK, N.Y. 10020
212 JU 6-1212

November 15, 1986

CHILI:

Two pounds of ground round.

Three cans of red kidney beans.

Three cans of tomato sauce.

Three tablespoons of chili con carne seasoning (Spice Islands).

Half tablespoon of chili powder.

Half tablespoon of ground cumin.

Two medium-sized onions chopped fine.

Brown meat and onions in heavy skillet or dutch oven, add beans
and tomato sauce, add spices and let simmer. For a hotter chili,
add more chili powder. This will serve up to ten persons.

But get them out of the house soon after eating.

Ron Fimrite, senior writer.

SPAGHETTI AND BRISKET

My Grandma Mast followed her husband to America, Land of Opportunity, from Poland in 1912. Unfortunately, the difference between NORTH America and SOUTH America became clear only after this small woman and her four children arrived in Buenos Aires. The family made an Argentine go of it until, now with seven children, they could afford to realize their dreams -- first in Chicago, then west in California.

As a kid growing up on the Monterey Peninsula, my summers were spent with Grandma in southern California, sniffing those wonderful smells from her ever-cooking kitchen. There was always a pot on the stove or in the oven -- often a Brisket -- a magical meat that would turn up in Kreplach or peeking out of mounds of spaghetti as in this recipe.

Beef brisket (make sure it's center cut, trimmed and "nice").
Rub with sliced garlic (5 cloves) and lotsa Spanish onions (3 or 4).
Put brisket, garlic and onions (pushed to side of meat) in roasting pan in oven.
Cook uncovered at 325 degrees until onions and meat are browned.

Don't turn meat. Cook an hour or more.
Then add water (a cup or more, depending) and cover.
Roast at 325 degrees for hours (maybe 2 or 3, depending).
When tender, remove meat and when cooler, slice against the grain for smoothness.

Add 2, 3, or 4 different kinds of cans of tomato sauce.
Taste; it may need a bit of sugar.
Cover and let it cook through.
Towards the end, add a nice bell pepper, cut in large chunks
    Should be cooked crisp, though.
Return meat to pan and heat through.
Serve with too much spaghetti.

Lloyd Firstman

The Gap, Inc.

900 Cherry Avenue
Post Office Box 60
San Bruno, CA 94066

Phone 415 952-4400
Telex 470224 GAP UI

Donald G. Fisher
Chairman and
Chief Executive Officer

APPLE CRISP

Peel, core and slice (very thin) or shred 5 or 6
cooking apples (green, if possible) into a pyrex
8-inch pie plate or baking dish.

```
Mix together well:  2   T. flour
                    1/2 C. sugar
                    1/2 t. cinnamon

          Add:  1 beaten egg
```

Fold this mixture into apples.

```
Combine:  1/4 C. butter
          2/3 C. flour
          1/3 C. brown sugar
```

with a fork until crumbly. (Chop across; do not
cream with flat part of fork.)

Sprinkle this mixture over the apple mixture.

Bake at 375 degrees until tender (about 40 minutes).
Raise temperature to 400 degrees for last 5 minutes
for a browner top.

Serve warm with whipped cream or soft ice cream
(or just plain).

84

M. F. K. FISHER 13935 Sonoma Highway Glen Ellen California 95442

PICKLED SEEDLESS GRAPES

Enough seedless grapes to make 3 or 4 c.
1½ c. granulated sugar
1 c. white wine vinegar
3 sticks cinnamon

Wash and stem grapes. Place in 3 clean ½pt. canning
jars. Bring sugar and vinegar to a boil and simmer
for 5 min. Pour syrup over grapes. Add 1 stick cinnamon
to each jar. Cover, and let stand overnight. Will be
ready to serve in 24 hrs., drained and chilled, with
cold meats, fish or roast fowl.

Seedless grapes, green or red, are best. If muscats or
Tokays are used, cut in half and seed. They have tougher
skins. Use soon, or store in a dark cool place, since
grapes will darken and toughen in Winter.

> Adapted from FINE PRESERVING
> Catherine Plageman
> Simon & Shuster, 1967 and
> Aris Books, 1986

I've always liked the San Francisco Ballet as perfect
entertainment. In the '50s and 60s I took my children
to it as much as possible, and my older girl worked
conscientiously for two years with Lew Christensen,
which, of course, made me feel only closer to it. And
since then, I have kept more than half an eye on it
through my friends who live nearer to it than I. By
now, my interest is more academic than active, but I
shall always think of it as an integral part of all
San Francisco life, a vital and important thing. I wish
that I could do more to help it in every possible way.
This present project seems to me like a fine way to
involve many people in keeping it alive and well.
Interest in it is really good, I know several hardworking
and hard-pressed creative people who would do much more
than copy out a recipe to help its survival. They all
want it to live forever, as do I, and if eating well is
a part of the San Francisco heritage, what better way
to keep the San Francisco Ballet alive than to stay
alive ourselves with good food?

Green Chicken

4 chicken breasts
2 13 oz Can Tomatillo (whole)
1 clove garlic
1 onion
2 bunches cilantro (stems removed)
16 oz container sour cream
3/4 lb jack cheese, grated
salt, to taste

Sauté onion and garlic

Put whole tomatillos, onion garlic and cilantro leaves in food processor turning on and off until ingredients are evenly chopped.

Simmer chicken until tender. Remove from the bones and separate breasts.

In a casserole, place chicken breasts, sauce, and put 2 tablespoons of sour cream on each piece chicken. Sprinkle with grated cheese until covered. Cook this dish at 350° for 40 minutes, or until all cheese melts. Serves 8-10.

Susan Verble Gantner

BREAST OF DUCK WITH MANGO SAUCE

1 Breast per serving
   season with salt and pepper
   sear in ½ butter and ½ oil
   then, roast in oven for 5-6 minutes for medium-rare
   remove meat from pan and set aside to rest, keeping warm
   degrease pan, reserving 1 tbsp. of drippings
   deglaze pan with white wine
   add: 2 tbsp. mango puree
        ½ tsp. cream
   check seasoning (salt & pepper)
   reduce to a sauce consistency
   finish with a little butter for proper flavor and consistency

MANGO BUTTER ROLLS

1 pint milk	2½ oz. yeast
1 pint mango puree	1¼ oz. salt
2 eggs	4 lb. 6 oz (approx.) bread flour

- Knead above ingredients together for 5 minutes.
  (hold back a small scoop of flour)

- Add: 13 oz butter and knead together for 15 minutes
        adjusting the flour as needed for a fairly firm dough.

- Divide the dough into desired size pieces   (1½ to 2 oz)
  for a normal size roll

- Shape and place on prepared sheet pans

- Proof until doubled in size

- Bake in 450 degree oven for approximately 20 minutes or
  until golden brown and done.

Roberto Gerometta
executive Chef

SQUARE ONE

POT LATCH SALMON

Have on hand one 6-8 oz. salmon filet per person.
Rub the following cure on the fish and let it marinate for at
least 3 hours.
Marinade: Combine 6 Tbsp. sugar
              2 Tbsp. Kosher salt
              3 Tbsp. ground juniper berries
              1 Tbsp. freshly ground black pepper
              optional- 2 Tbsp. orange zest, grated

This marinade is enough for six portions of fish, approximately.

Heat broiler or start fire in barbeque or grill.
When the grill or broiler is very hot,brush salmon with a little olive
oil, and then grill a few minutes on each side, til salmon is medium rare
to medium. Serve with a lemon wedge and sauteed spinach or swiss chard.

I love this recipe because it is so simple and so very tasty.
The fish developes a delicate sweetness; the hint of juniper adds
a perfume of gin without the kick. This dish is not rich , and is
perfect for those who want to eat light, but eat well.

Joyce Goldstein

THE RESTAURANT AT
GOLDEN GATEWAY COMMONS
190 PACIFIC AT FRONT
SAN FRANCISCO 94111
TELEPHONE 415 788-1110

CARY GOTT
Executive Vice President
Winemaster

MAYONNAISE KISSES

When I was a child, my parents had me pass these delicious hors d'oeuvres to guests at cocktail parties they frequently hosted for Modesto "Society". I usually passed them until one or two were remaining on the tray. Then I would return to the kitchen for more (and, of course, eat what was left on the tray).

A few years ago, I gave them the name 'Mayonnaise Kisses', and in honor of them, I obtained a personalized license plate for my Porsche that reads "MANAZE".

I love to eat them--they are outstanding!

Best Foods or Hellman's Mayonnaise (do not substitute)
White boiling onions - 1" diameter
Paprika
Regular white bread

Use a 2" round cookie cutter to cut out 4 rounds per slice of bread with no crusts.

Peel and thinly slice (1/8"-1/4") the onions, and put one onion round on top of each round of the white bread.

Put a dollop of Mayonnaise on top of the onion, and sprinkle lightly with paprika.

Preheat broiler.

Broil on cookie sheet 6"-8" from heat (about 1-2 minutes).

Serve warm.

Cary Gott

BILL GRAHAM PRESENTS

There's a favorite snack that I always enjoy, and it's a standard item in my refrigerator. The key item is Aoli, a garlic mayonnaise, which is used as a dip for fresh vegetables or seafood. It's simple to make and absolutely delicious. Here's the recipe:

AOLI

3 egg yolks
6 cloves garlic - pressed
1/2 tsp. salt
1 Tblsp. lemon juice
1/2 cup olive oil
1/2 cup vegetable oil
Up to 1 Tblsp. of water

In a blender, combine the egg yolks, crushed garlic, salt and lemon juice. Blend.

Mix the two oils together and then slowly - drop by drop - add the oil to the blender while the blender is running.

Add up to one tablespoon of water to obtain the consistency you prefer for dip.

Enjoy!

Cheers!

Bill Graham

Bill Graham

P.O. Box 1994, San Francisco, CA 94101   415/864-0815

THE DIET WOMEN NEED MOST

ENCHILADAS

- 1 teaspoon diet margarine
- ¼ cup chopped scallions
- 1 large clove garlic, crushed
- ¼ teaspoon ground cumin
- 1 pound ground turkey
- 10 6-inch corn tortillas
- 2 14½-ounce cans low-sodium stewed tomatoes
- 1 4-ounce can chopped green chilies, drained
- ½ cup grated part-skim mozzarella cheese
- 2 tablespoons chopped fresh parsley, optional

Heat oven to 350° F. In large skillet over medium heat, melt margarine; add scallions, garlic and cumin; cook 1 minute, stirring until vegetables are coated with cumin. Add turkey; cook about 5 minutes until meat loses raw color, stirring with fork to break up. Meanwhile, wrap tortillas in foil; place in oven to soften and heat through. Drain one can stewed tomatoes, reserving juice. Add drained tomatoes to turkey mixture along with chilies; cook about 10 minutes, stirring frequently. If mixture appears too dry, add up to 2 tablespoons reserved tomato juice. Stir in ¼ cup mozzarella; remove from heat. Set aside to cool slightly. Meanwhile, drain remaining can stewed tomatoes; chop roughly. Place tomatoes in 1-quart saucepan; cook over medium heat about 5 minutes until heated through. *To assemble:* Remove tortillas from oven; maintain oven temperature. Fill each softened tortilla with generous ¼ cup

turkey mixture; roll up; place on ovenproof serving platter or baking dish. Pour hot tomato sauce over tortillas; sprinkle with remaining ¼ cup mozzarella. Place in oven about 5 minutes until heated through and cheese is melted. Sprinkle with parsley, if desired. Makes 5 servings.

One of my favorites !

Joanie

PRODUCED BY JOANIE GREGGAINS PRODUCTIONS
201 MILLER AVENUE
MILL VALLEY, CA
94941

DISTRIBUTED BY PSS
Program Syndication Services Inc.
A SUBSIDIARY OF DANCER FITZGERALD SAMPLE, INC.
405 LEXINGTON AVENUE, NEW YORK, NY 10174
(212) 532-1560

NATIONAL SALES OFFICE GROUP W TV SALES
90 PARK AVENUE
18TH FLOOR
NEW YORK, NY 10016

91

207 Powell Street, 6th Floor
San Francisco, California 94102-2252   (415) 392-9175
Artists' Manager, Casting for T.V., Motion Pictures, Radio, Print, Fashion Shows, SAG, AFTRA & SEG

BAKED PORK CHOPS STUFFED
WITH OYSTER DRESSING

serves 8

Ingredients

- 8 pork chops, 2 inches thick (have your butcher cut a pocket on the meaty side about 2x2 for dressing)

- 1 package herbed croutons

- 1 glass jar of oysters with liquid (canned oysters will work)

- 1 small green apple, peeled, cored, and chopped

- 1 small onion, chopped

- 3 stalks celery, chopped

- 1 tablespoon poultry seasoning

- 1 teaspoon sage

- salt and pepper to taste

Method

- Mix croutons and oyster liquid to moisten— add extra water or wine if necessary.

- Add onions, apple, celery, poultry seasoning, sage, and salt and pepper.

- Divide dressing evenly among pork chops and stuff into cavities.

- Place into "Pammed" shallow pan, uncovered, in oven at 350° for 1 hour.

Serve with apple sauce and tossed green salad.

MRS. WALTER A. HAAS, JR.

2666 BROADWAY   SAN FRANCISCO, CALIFORNIA 94115

Sparerib Sauce
A Favorite of the Family - All Ages

1 stick or 1/2 cup butter
3/4 cup catsup
1/2 cup brown sugar
3 Tablespoons lemon juice
1 Tablespoon Dijon style mustard
2 teaspoons each of bottled steak sauce, hot
    pepper sauce (Tabasco), and Worcestershire
    sauce

Melt butter in saucepan. Stir in catsup, brown
sugar, lemon juice, mustard, steak, pepper, and
Worcestershire sauce.

We always put our ribs in a 375° oven for one half
hour before putting on the sauce. This eliminates
some of the sparerib's grease and fat. Therefore,
to barbecue spareribs, first place in oven for half
hour and then brush the ribs with sauce. Finally
put on grill and keep turning and basting. Cook
for 45 minutes.

Lemon Hits
A Treat and Addictive!

1 cup flour
1/2 cup butter
1/4 cup powdered sugar

Heat oven to 350°. Blend flour, butter and
powdered sugar. Thoroughly mix and pat into an
8-inch square pan, slightly buttered. Bake at 350°
for 20 minutes.

2 eggs
1 cup sugar
3 Tablesppons lemon juice
1/4 teaspoon salt
1/2 teaspoon baking powder

Beat rest of ingredients together. Pour over crust
and bake 20-25 minutes more. Do not overbake, (top
should be slightly brown). The filling puffs
during baking but flattens when cool.

Evelyn D. Haas

Prentis Cobb Hale

150 Stockton Street, San Francisco, CA 94108

FRICASSEE OF CHICKEN   (Serves 6)

A rich, creamy chicken stew and a useful dish for entertaining
because, except for the final cream and egg yolk enrichment, it
can be completed in advance and loses none of its special qualities
when heated again. Serve with rice and a green vegetable.

```
5 to 6 pounds cut-up frying chicken
4 tablespoons (1/2 stick) butter
2 cups finely chopped onion
2 cloves garlic, minced
1 bay leaf
1/4 teaspoon ground nutmeg
3 tablespoons chopped fresh tarragon, OR
        2 teaspoons dried tarragon
1 teaspoon chopped fresh thyme, OR
        1/2 teaspoon dried thyme
1/4 teaspoon cayenne pepper
Salt and freshly ground pepper
1 cup chicken broth
1 cup dry white wine
1/2 cup flour
2 cups heavy cream
3 egg yolks
2 tablespoons lemon juice
Chopped parsley OR additional chopped fresh tarragon
```

Pull off and discard the skin from the chicken pieces--thus ridding
the chicken of most of its fat. Heat butter in a large casserole or
Dutch oven over moderate heat. When it is foaming, add the chicken,
then the onion, garlic, bay leaf, nutmeg, tarragon, thyme and
cayenne. Stir to combine thoroughly, then season lightly with salt
and pepper. Cook, stirring almost constantly over moderate heat
for about 5 to 7 minutes, until the onion is wilted and the chicken
has lost its squashy raw texture. Sprinkle with the flour and cook,
stirring, for about 3 minutes longer. Add the chicken broth and
wine and stir well to incorporate every bit of the flour and make a
smooth sauce. Bring to a gentle boil, cover the pot, reduce heat,
and simmer gently for about 15 to 20 minutes, until chicken is
cooked through.

Blend the cream and egg yolks together in a small bowl. Add to the
hot chicken and bring back to a simmer, stirring, but do not boil
or the egg yolks will scramble. Stir in the lemon juice. Arrange
the chicken pieces on a large warm serving platter, then pour the
sauce over and sprinkle parsley or tarragon over all.

Prentis Cobb Hale

938 Coral Drive, Pebble Beach, California

Mousse au Chocolat

4 1-ounce squares bitter chocolate
1/4 cup water
3/4 cup sugar
5 eggs
2 Tablespoons dark rum

Melt the chocolate in the top of a double boiler. Add water and sugar and stir until the sugar is dissolved. Separate the yolks from the whites. Add the yolks, one by one, beating vigorously. Remove from heat and add the rum. Beat the egg whites stiff and fold into the chocolate mixture. Pour into individual molds or a dessert bowl and place in the refrigerator. Let it stand for at least 12 hours; the longer it chills, the better it is. It will keep for several days. Serve with whipped cream.

Makes 6 large servings

This dessert is incredibly easy to make and just as incredibly delicious.

Laurie H. Hall

Grilled Swordfish with a Tomato Coulis and Tarragon

6-8oz. Swordfish
2 Tomatoes
1/4 Tsp. Lemon Juice

1 Bunch Tarragon
1/4 cup Olive Oil

1. Slice Swordfish into 1/2 inch Steaks. Place onto Sheet Pan. Coat with Olive Oil and Season.
2. Remove Core from Tomatoes, squeeze excess water from Tomatoes and Puree' with Food Processor. Strain to remove seeds.
3. Add 1 Tbsp. Olive Oil, Lemon Juice, and Tarragon. to Tomato Puree'. Season to taste.
4. Grill Swordfish over hot fire. Preference Medium Rare.
5. Place Sauce on warm plate. Next Swordfish and top fish with Tarragon leaves.

RESTAURANT 101

RED SNAPPER IN WINE SAUCE

1 stick of sweet butter
1/3 bottle of red wine (approximately 8 ounces)
2 Tablespoons chopped shallots
2 Tablespoons of cream
Salt
White Pepper

2 bunches of fresh spinach

4 filets of Red Snapper, Halibut, Sole or any white fish

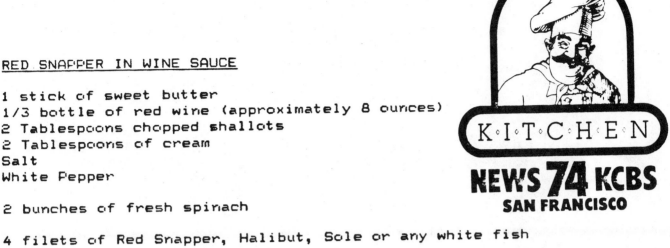

Place the shallots and red wine in a small saucepan and reduce over a high heat until you have about 1/3 of a cup of liquid. While the wine is reducing, bring a lot of water to the boil to blanch the spinach. I like to wash the spinach as a whole bunch. Move the twist tie down the stems away from the leaves and tighten it. Wash in a basin of luke-warm water or with the sprayer. Dip the spinach into the boiling water by the stems just enough to wilt it. Let it drain in a colander, then squeeze it dry. Cut off the stems and divide into four piles. You'll want them to be about the size of your hand, or a little bit bigger than the filets of fish.

When the wine is sufficiently reduced, add the cream and cook it a bit more. The finished sauce will be as thick as this mixture, so if you want a thick sauce, reduce it some more, otherwise leave it on the thin side. The acid in the red wine can cause the sauce to break, so don't overdo it. Add all but a pat of the butter, bit by bit to the sauce as you whisk it over a low heat. The butter should be cold as you add it and only add the butter as fast as it incorporates into the sauce. Take the sauce off the heat and season it with salt and white pepper.

Season the fish lightly with salt and pepper. With the remaining pat of butter in a large no-stick pan, saute the fish filets over a medium heat. Cook on both sides for only 30 seconds and then crowd them to one side of the pan. Place the piles of spinach in the pan and place the filets on each pile of spinach. Cover the pan and let steam for about 2 minutes - long enough to cook the fish and warm the spinach.

Warm the serving plates and place a pool of the red wine sauce in the bottom of each plate. Place a spinach and fish pile on top.

Mussels with Extra Virgin olive oil,
Lemon and garlic

for 4-6 people:

15-18 mussels per person, washed

8-10T extra virgin olive oil

2 cloves garlic, finely minced

4 T Lemon juice, preferably
from Meyer Lemons

in a large sauté pan place
oil, lemon, garlic and mussels -
cover and cook over a low flame
until the mussels open about
4-5 minutes

serve with good bread -

Anne Haskel
Partner + chef

TUNA ITALIANO

This dish is good for those evenings when you come
home after a long rehearsal and find the refrigerator
empty. We try to keep these ingredients on the shelf.

1 can (7 oz.) tuna fish, drained
1 can (1 lb. 12 oz.) Italian peeled tomatoes with basil
1/3 cup olive oil
2 large cloves garlic, finely chopped
1 teaspoon oregano
Several fresh basil leaves, chopped (if available)
Salt and pepper
1 lb. pasta (Linguine is best)

In a saucepan, saute garlic in oil until light golden.
Chop tomatoes. (You can do this in the can with a sharp
knife or scissors.) Add tomatoes and oregano to oil and
garlic. Cook for 30 minutes over low heat. Cook pasta.
Just before pasta is done, add tuna to sauce, salt and
pepper to taste. Put well-drained pasta in heated bowl,
add sauce and sprinkle with chopped basil. Serves three
theatre folk or four normal people.

Edward Hastings
Artistic Director

SHORENSTEIN HAYS ☆ NEDERLANDER ORGANIZATION

CURRAN THEATRE
GOLDEN GATE THEATRE
ORPHEUM THEATRE

CAROLE SHORENSTEIN HAYS

THE POST OPENING NIGHT SPECIAL

1 package of Oscar Mayer Bologna
1 package of Velveeta "Single Slice" Cheese
Wonder White Bread
Mayonnaise
Celestial Seasonings Lemon Zinger Tea (Caffeine Free)
3-5 Video Classics (preferably Hepburn and Tracy)
1 down comforter

Take 2 pieces of plain white bread. Slice off crust. Spread
mayonnaise generously. Place 2 to 3 slices of bologna
on one side of bread. Place 1 to 2 slices of Velveeta atop
the bologna. Place the other slice of bread atop the velveeta and bologna slice. Cut diagonally to make 4 triangular
sandwiches. Dip 1 bag of Lemon Zinger Tea into a large
cup of boiling water. Let sit for 3 minutes. Place your
favorite movie in the VCR. Press Play. Settle into a
thick down comforter with your bologna and velveeta
sandwich and tea beside you. Take the phone off the hook
and enjoy!

ROULADES   4 people

4 slices of thin cut beef
(round or flank steak)

you may pound the meat

coat one side with mustard

add 2 strips of thin cut bacon on top
of the mustard

add 1 finely chopped small sized dill
pickle to each slice

roll the meat with content

secure each roll with 2 toothpicks or
tie with string (remove toothpicks or
string before serving)

brown Roulades vigorously on all sides
in bacon grease with 2 onions (make sure
onions are browned well at the same time)

add beef stock or consommé

add red wine

let simmer for 1 hour and 15 minutes

(the amount of liquid used depends on
how much gravy is desired)

serve with red cabbage and spaetzle or
noodles.

Ingrid Hills

P. S. The above recipe is the only
"foolproof" dish I can whip
together without much agony
and satisfaction guaranteed!
It is tasty, simple and
filling and invariably puts
a smile on my husband's
face.

ARTHUR HOPPE

Nov. 17, 1986

Manx Ghlum

Take 1 slice of bread and lay it flat on counter top or similar structure. Place jelly on bread. Spread carefully, making sure not to go over edges. Place peanut butter on other slice of bread. Spread carefully, making sure that the entire surface is covered and no "white spots" remain. Now, with quick motion, flip the slice with the peanut butter on top of the slice bearing the jelly. UNDER NO CIRCUMSTANCE attempt to flip the slice bearing the jelly on top of the slice that is peanut-buttered. Serves 1.

SAN FRANCISCO CHRONICLE • SAN FRANCISCO • CALIFORNIA 94119 • (415) 777-1111

JOHN B. HUNTINGTON
ATTORNEY AT LAW
P. O. BOX 1006
TIBURON, CALIFORNIA 94920
(415) 435-4440

QUAIL AND OYSTERS

Serves 4
Cooking Time 30 Minutes

4 quail

8 oysters

1/2 cube sweet butter

1/2 cup fresh bread crumbs

1/2 cup dry white wine

Salt, pepper and sage to taste

2 teaspoons black caviar

4 small pieces pimiento

Bone the quail

Melt the butter

Season the fresh bread crumbs with pepper and sage

Preheat the oven to 350 degrees. Dip each oyster in the melted butter and then in the seasoned bread crumbs. Stuff each quail with 2 oysters and sew up the quail. Arrange quail in a shallow pan and brush them with melted butter. Roast the quail at 350 degrees for 15 minutes. Pour dry white wine over the top and roast another 15 minutes at 350 degrees. Serve garnished with black caviar and pimiento.

This old Louisiana plantation recipe provides a happy combination of two unique flavors.

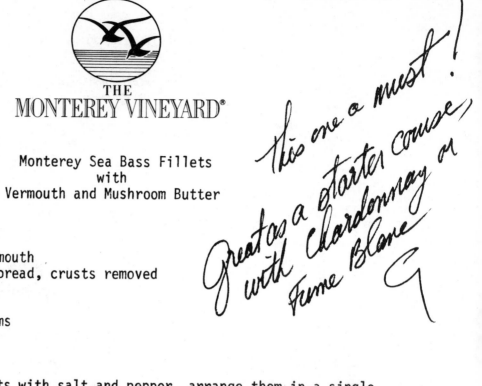

THE MONTEREY VINEYARD®

GARY IBSEN
Director of Public Relations

Monterey Sea Bass Fillets
with
Vermouth and Mushroom Butter

6 fillets of Sea Bass
Fresh ground pepper
1/4 cup plus 2 T. Vermouth
2 thick slices white bread, crusts removed
16 T. unsalted butter
2 T. chopped parsley
2/3 lb. fresh mushrooms
1T. fresh lemon juice
1 T. water

Season the fish fillets with salt and pepper, arrange them in a single layer in a large buttered baking dish and drizzle vermouth over them. Place the bread in the container of a food processor or blender and process to make fine crumbs.

Place 7 T. of the butter in mixing bowl to soften. Add the bread crumbs and beat until well blended. Preheat oven to 450 degrees.
Meanwhile trim, rinse and drain the mushrooms and cut into thin slices.

In a small saucepan combine the mushrooms, lemon juice, 1 T. of the remaining butter and water. Season with salt and pepper. Bring to a boil over medium heat and boil for 1 minute. Remove the mushrooms from the broth with a slotted spoon, set aside and keep warm. Reduce the mushroom broth over medium heat until only 3 T. of liquid remain.

Place the fish in the hot oven and bake for 5 - 7 minutes. Meanwhile, finish the mushroom butter: Cut the remaining 8 T. butter in small pieces and whisk them, one at a time into the reduced mushroom broth over low heat. Remove the fillets from the oven and pour any juices from the bottom of the pan into the mushroom butter.

It not serving immediately, keep the fish, the mushrooms, and the mushroom butter warm in separate dishes. Spread a thin layer of the bread crumb mixture over the top of each fillet, patting it down gently to the fish.

Just before serving, place the fillets under the broiler for 2 minutes until lightly browned. Spoon a little mushroom butter on the bottom of 6 serving plates. Arrange a bouquet of mushrooms larger than fillets on each plate. Using a spatula, carefully place browned fillets on the serving plates on top of mushrooms.

Although I was born, brought up and trained in my native France; I never cease to marvel at the new discoveries of taste sensations which I continually uncover in the new world. This little recipe is a variation of a basic Mexican salsa theme which brings together fruit and tomatoes and chiles and cilantro. All ingredients harmonize so as to bring forth the texture goodness of a fresh broiled sea bass. Innovative of itself, the salsa with fruit is an unusual accent for this popular seafood.

BROILED SEA BASS WITH ORANGE-PINEAPPLE SALSA

INGREDIENTS:

For each serving:
1 6-ounce fresh filet of sea bass
1 tablespoon unsalted butter, melted
1 cilantro sprig, for garnish

Orange-Pineapple Salsa (serves 8):
1 tomato, peeled
½ bunch cilantro
2 oranges, peeled and sectioned
1 small onion
1 cup fresh pineapple chunks
8 Serrano chiles
¼ cup vegetable oil
½ teaspoon freshly ground black pepper

PROCEDURE:

Make the salsa a few hours ahead. Dice all the fruit and vegetables except the chiles to the same size. Chop the chiles, with their seeds in, very fine. Mix all the ingredients together and set aside until ready to serve.

Broil (or grill) the fish filets. Place one filet on each dinner plate and brush with melted butter. Spoon a generous amount of salsa over the fish. Garnish with a cilantro sprig. Serve with a sliced boiled potato and your choice of vegetables.

Bon Appetit,

Christian Iser
Executive Chef d'Cuisine

MARINATED CRAB

Ingredients

2 large live Dungeness crabs

Marinade: 1 cup olive oil
              ½ cup <u>fresh</u> lime juice
              2 medium cloves garlic, peeled and minced
              ¼ cup small capers
              ¼ cup stuffed green olives, finely chopped
              ½ cup sun dried tomatoes, finely chopped
              1 large bunch cilantro, cleaned, trimmed and chopped
              ½ medium red onion, peeled and finely chopped
              ¼ tsp red pepper flakes (or to taste)

1. Clean, crack and steam crabs for 5 minutes or until the crabmeat
    turns opaque.
2. Mince the olives, tomatoes, cilantro and onions.
3. In a bowl, add the olive oil. Mix in the lime juice and then add
    the minced ingredients. Add capers and mix thoroughly. Adjust
    marinade for sharpness, hotness. Add freshly ground pepper and
    salt to taste.
4. Let the crab cool. While just warm, put the crab in a large bowl
    with a cover. Pour the marinade over the crab and cover, turning
    every hour or so to redistribute the marinade.
5. Marinate for at least six hours or overnight. Serve on chilled
    leaves of lettuce and garnish with lime slices and black olives.
    Accompany with a fresh, local baguette and a crisp, dry white wine.

JEANNE-MAR

moira johnston

HARVEST STEW-IN-A-PUMPKIN   (Serves 6 to 8)

It was the Wine Institute's annual prizewinning recipe, and it
sounded wonderful. A harvest stew served at table in a pumpkin!
I served it up to visiting guests, including the former Prime
Minister of Canada. The pumpkin shell was alarmingly soft and
slumped as I took it from the oven, and I prayed as I carried it
to the table. But as I began to ladle the stew onto steaming
polenta, the pumpkin gave way like a levee crumbling before a
flood. And, to cries of alarm, the stew gushed out and spread
over the table. I frantically encircled the flood with dishtowels
and, luckily, had reserves in a pot on the stove. It was the most
dramatic dinner party since the Christmas when the flaming plum
pudding licked fire up my arms, slid from the platter, and rolled
down the table like a fiery cannon ball.

1 large pumpkin (10 to 12 lbs.)
6 tblsp. oil
2 lbs. lean beef, cubed
1 cup flour
½ tsp. salt
1 tsp. pepper
½ cup brandy
1 cup coarse chopped onion
1 cup green pepper, chopped
4 garlic cloves, minced
3 cups beef stock
1 cup dry red wine

3 chopped tomatoes
2 bay leaves
1 tsp. oregano
1½ lb. cubed potatoes
1 lb. sweet potatoes, thick sliced
1 lb. zucchini, thick sliced
3 ears fresh corn
16 dried pitted prunes
1 cup brown sugar
½ cup butter
4 tsps. cinnamon

Toss beef in flour, salt and pepper. Coat and shake off. Brown in
4 tblsps. oil, add brandy, stir, reserve on platter. In same pan,
put rest of oil, onions, pepper, garlic, and cook until soft. Add
beef stock and wine, bring to boil, scrape pan. Return meat and
juices to pan. Stir in tomatoes, bay leaf and oregano. Cover and
simmer on low heat for 15 minutes. Add potatoes and cook covered
for 15 minutes more. Add corn, cook covered for 5 minutes. Add
zucchini and prunes, cook for 3 minutes. Simmer on low heat for
one hour.

Heat oven to 375 degrees.

Prepare pumpkin: Scrape pumpkin clean of seeds and fiber. Brush
liberally with melted butter, sprinkle with sugar and cinnamon,
place pumpkin on well-greased pan, and bake 45 minutes. Watch to
make sure shell is still firm! Pour pumpkin juices into stew, and
ladle stew into pumpkin. Bake 15 minutes, shift carefully to serving platter. Scrape pumpkin flesh as you ladle stew. Festive, aro-
matic and delicious. Serve with polenta and a rich
zinfandel or cabernet. Bon appetit!

moira johnston

CHICKEN PONAPE
by Proctor "Chook"* Jones, Jr.

Serves 6

Ingredients:

6 half breasts chicken, boned and skinned
20 oz. fresh linguini
1/2 lb. mushrooms, sliced
5 cloves garlic, finely chopped
3 teaspoons ginger root, finely grated
1 head broccoli
6 oz prepared pesto sauce
6 oz grated parmesan cheese
1 pint Half and Half
1 cup white wine
1/2 stick butter
2 and 1/2 teaspoons olive oil
2 and 1/2 Tablespoons Dijon mustard
1/2 teaspoon oregano
salt
pepper

1. Steam the broccoli till just cooked, still crunchy. After steaming, chop coarsely and set aside.

2. Melt butter in large saucepan and saute breasts with garlic, ginger, mustard, and salt and pepper to taste. Cooking over medium heat, add wine gradually. Add mushrooms and oregano near the end of sauteing.

3. Boil and drain noodles al dente. Toss with olive oil to separate strands. Add parmesan, Half and Half, and broccoli to pasta. Add pesto.

4. Remove chicken and slice into 1/2 inch strips. Pour remaining liquid from pan into pasta. Place sliced chicken over mixture and serve.

*Means chicken in Australia

108

ROBERT TRENT JONES, JR.

My travels around the world began many years ago in the Pacific Rim when I was working on new golf course projects in the Philippines, Hawaii, Japan, and Thailand. I discovered an American dish with a sweet flavor, zestfully enriched with fruits of Hawaii. I call it Hawaiian Spareribs.

HAWAIIAN SPARERIBS

pork spareribs (about 1 lb. per person)
bar-b-que sauce (I use Kraft)
honey
crushed pineapple
sesame seeds

Line a roasting pan with foil. Spread the ribs in the pan, coat them with bar-b-que sauce, then cover with honey. Spoon crushed pineapple over them and sprinkle with sesame seeds. Broil in the oven for ½ hour. Take them out of the oven, turn the ribs over and cover them with the same ingredients. Return them to the oven for another ½ hour. The ribs will be blackened, crunchy and delicious!

Aloha!

Robert Trent Jones J

WOODSIDE, CALIFORNIA 94062

109

Fleur De Lys
Restaurant Francais
777 Sutter Street, San Francisco, CA 94109
(415) 673-7779

BELUGA CAVIAR, SEA URCHIN AND ASPARAGUS IN A LIGHT PUFF PASTRY SHELL

Le Feuillete Leger aux Oursins, Caviar Beluga
et Pointes D'Asperges Vertes

DEGREE OF DIFFICULTY: Medium
PRICE   : Expensive
TIME NEEDED   : 35 Minutes
SERVES   : 4

INGREDIENTS:

4 teaspoons Beluga Caviar
4 Sea Urchin (small size)
2 dz. cooked asparagus tips (pencil asparagus)
5 large eggs
1 egg yolk
1 tablespoon finely cut chives
1 ounce butter
3 ounces heavy cream
½ bunch watercress
6 oz. puff pastry dough

PREPARATION:

To open the sea urchin: the bottom or mouth side of the sea
urchin is slightly flattened. You can cut a section out of
the side with scissors and dump the roe out, or scoop it out
with a teaspoon. Heat the oven to 400°F.

On a lightly floured surface, roll the dough to 1/8" thickness.
With a pie cutter (2½ inches) cut 8 circles and put 4 of them
on a greased and lightly floured baking sheet. Brush the
pastries with one egg yolk beaten with a spoonful of water.
With a pie cutter (1 inch) cut 4 circles in the center of the
4 remaining pastries. With the 4 obtained rings, top the 2½ inch
circles. Bake in a 400°F oven for 15 to 20 minutes. The dough
should have browned nicely. With a small sharp knife take out
the center of the puff pastry shell. Keep them warm.

Fleur De Lys

Restaurant Francais
777 Sutter Street, San Francisco, CA 94109
(415) 673-7779

(continued)

Meanwhile wash the watercress and trim off the leaves. Discard the stems. Bring 3 oz. of salted cream to a boil. Add the leaves and boil for 4 minutes. Blend the mixture for one minute and you will obtain a light watercress cream sauce. Season to taste. Scramble the 5 large eggs, keeping them soft and stir in one ounce of butter, the chopped chives and the sea urchin roe.

Mix well and season with salt and pepper.

Spoon a layer of watercress sauce into the center of each plate. Arrange the puff pastry shells on top. Arrange the pre-heated asparagus tips around the plate. Garnish the shells with the sea urchin, scrambled eggs and top each one with a teaspoon of Beluga Caviar.

The sea urchin roe has a delicious, delicate flavor that could be described as "sea with a hint of melon." The darker the roe, the more pronounced the flavor.

HUBERT KELLER
Chef de Cuisine

Matthew E.G. Kelly
358 Lombard Street
San Francisco 94133
415-362 0544

BUTTERFLY LEG OF LAMB ET AL

This recipe will suffice for a complete dinner--is easy to prepare, attractive to present and should inspire the most jaded palate.

Have your butcher butterfly a medium leg of lamb trimming excess fat and muscle so that the meat will tend to be of uniform thickness. You will also need:

> One cup bulgur (coarse ground wheat)
> Red and green peppers
> Fresh garlic cloves
> One quart chicken stock

> For marinade

> ¼ cup of ginger
> ¼ cup of Coleman's dry mustard
> ¼ cup of coarse brown sugar
> One cup of red wine
> Salt & pepper to taste

Briskly rub the meat with fresh garlic cloves and then marinate for three hours.

Place one cup of bulgar in a hot frying pan well coated with olive oil until all grains are toasted a golden brown (usually about 5 minutes). Stir occasionally to prevent burning. When the bulgur is toasted, add one quart of chicken stock and place in a 350° oven for 30 minutes, stirring occasionally.

Cook the lamb over hot coals, skin down until the upper side is warm to the touch then turn, baste, and grill the top side equally. This should give a charcoal pink look to the slices when served.

Slice two or three red and green peppers, steam briefly then saute in olive oil and garlic.

Slice the lamb, coat with marinade and present on a warmed plate with bulgur bordered with the peppers for a dash of color. Serve with garlic bread. Voila! A treat for the gourmand.

Hank Ketcham
Enterprises, Inc
P.O. Box 800, Pebble Beach, Calif. 93953
(408) 625-3130

OMELET CREPES WITH CRABMEAT

2 TABLESPOONS FLOUR
3 EGGS
1/2 CUP LIGHT CREAM
PINCH OF SALT
DASH OF PEPPER
BUTTER
1 CUP CANNED CRABMEAT

Put flour into mixing bowl and with a whisk, beat in eggs one at a time. Add cream, salt and pepper, then stir batter until smooth.

Heat 5" heavy cast-iron skillet until very hot. Coat with soft butter. Remove skillet from heat, pour in generous tablespoon of batter. Quickly tilt and rotate pan so batter runs to the edges, coating bottom of pan thinly and evenly.

Return pan to heat for just a minute or two. When the top of the crepe is set and the bottom golden brown, lift with spatula and carefully remove to a cooling rack. As you finish cooking the remaining crepes, pile them on top of each other with a sheet of wax paper between each crepe.

Distribute a generous tablespoon of crabmeat on the uncooked side of each crepe, then wrap the crepe around the filling.

Allow two crepes per person. (This recipe makes about 12 crepes.) Anoint with Russian dressing and sprinkle with chopped parsley.

Hank Ketcham

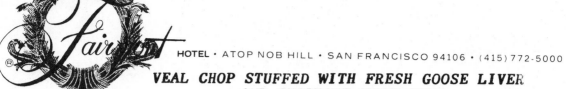

VEAL CHOP STUFFED WITH FRESH GOOSE LIVER AND SHIITAKE MUSHROOMS
Serves 4 people

Ingredients

4 clean veal chops (6 to 8 oz. each)
4 slices of fresh goose livers (1 oz. each)
1 lb. fresh shiitake mushrooms
3 pieces fresh shallots (chopped)
4 tbsp. fresh butter
½ cup chablis wine
Fresh thyme and bay leaves
Salt and pepper

MOREL SAUCE

8 pieces of dry smoked morels
1 piece fresh shallot
¼ cup Cognac
1 cup heavy cream
½ cup veal gravy
1 tsp. fresh butter

Vegetables and starch

Fresh asparagus
Fresh tomato pasta

Preparation

Remove the fat and the silver skin off the veal chop
Cut an incision on the side of the chop big enough to stuff the sliced goose liver in
Chop the shiitake mushrooms (very small)
Saute with 2 tbsp. of butter and 3 pieces chopped shallots
Add thyme, bay leaves, salt, pepper and then the wine
Cook at very low heat to puree consistency
Cool the puree then stuff the veal chop with puree and goose liver. The goose liver should be between layers of puree
Season with salt and pepper and a little thyme
Saute the veal chops in a teflon pan with 1 tbsp. fresh butter
Cook rare
Remove the chop from pan and keep in a warm place
Add 1 tbsp. butter to the pan, then saute the soaked morels with with 1 chopped shallot (Soak the morels in warm water and rinse twice, chop, then use as directed)
Saute and flambe with the Cognac
Add the heavy cream, reduce to ½
Add ½ cup brown veal gravy
Season with salt and pepper
Serve with fresh asparagus and fresh tomato pasta

Created by Kurt Kratschmar (Executive Chef)
Fairmont Hotel and Tower
San Francisco

THE FAIRMONT HOTELS. DALLAS · DENVER · NEW ORLEANS · SAN FRANCISCO
SAN JOSE. CALIFORNIA OPENING FALL 1987
CHICAGO. ILLINOIS OPENING FALL 1987

114   For information or reservations at any Fairmont Hotel, call Toll Free 800-527-4727

MATILDA KUNIN'S ACTOR'S RED PEPPER SOUP
can be served hot or cold

tremendous for a quick pick-up

serves 4 - 6

INGREDIENTS:

7 red peppers
3 carrots (peeled)
3 shallots (peeled)
1 garlic clove (peeled)
1 pear (peeled)
1 T. olive oil
1/2 stick unsalted butter
1 quart chicken stock
1 T. crushed, dried red pepper
dash cayenne pepper
salt and black pepper to taste
sprig of tarragon
dollop of sour cream

STEPS

1. Slice 6 red peppers, carrots, shallots, garlic, and pear.

2. Heat oil and butter in skillet and saute vegetables and pear for 10 minutes over medium heat.

3. Add stock, dried red pepper, cayenne pepper, salt and pepper. Bring to boil and simmer with cover for 30 minutes.

4. While soup is cooking, roast remaining red pepper over direct heat until completely charred. Wash off blackened skin under cold water and remove seeds. Drain on paper towel.

5. Puree soup in blender adding roasted red pepper. Pour pureed soup back into pan and reheat over low flame.

6. Garnish with tarragon and a dollop of sour cream.

RICHARD A. KUNIN, M.D.
2698 PACIFIC AVENUE
SAN FRANCISCO, CALIFORNIA 94115

TELEPHONE: (415) 346-2500

CELEBRITY COOK BOOK

CRISIS DIET   by Richard A. Kunin, M.D.

Now that you have had your fill of gourmet eating, you may
be in dire need of immediate nutrient and weight control.
The **CRISIS DIET** is designed to provide adequate nutrients
and minimal calories at very moderate cost. It is practical
for periods of up to 3 weeks and weight loss of ten pounds
or more is usual. The use of linseed oil with this recipe
provides a rich source of health protecting omega 3 oils,
comparable to those found in fish oil but better tasting.

INCREDIENTS:

1. Soy protein powder (80% protein), 2 Tbsp

2. Non-fat milk, 8 oz.

3. Lite salt, 1/3 tsp

4. Linseed oil, 1 tsp

INSTRUCTIONS:

Flavor with 1 tsp Cocoa, 2 tsp molasses or ½ tsp Swiss Miss
Chocolate Milk Maker (with aspartame). Coffee may be substituted for milk to vary flavor--and further reduce calories.
Three servings per day provide about 700 calories. For best
health a two-a-day type multivitamin-mineral tablet should
be taken with each serving. If constipation occurs, add a
300 mg tablet of magnesium oxide. NOTE: The addition of
1 carrot and 3 stalks of celery is sensible. This is also
useful taken just once or twice daily for lesser crises.

This recipe is my personal rendition of that fine dish, Poulet Saute a la Bordelaise, from the French Provincial repertoire. My first sight of the artichoke fields in Castroville, California, reminded me of this dish, bringing back memories of my childhood in France.

POULET SAUTE A LA BORDELAISE

Serves 4

INGREDIENTS:

2   2½-pound yellow chickens, cut into quarters, boneless
6   large artichoke bottoms, cooked, choke removed, cut into quarters
24 small shallots, peeled
2   cups high-quality chicken broth
2   cups dry white wine (Sauvignon, if possible)
½   cup Cognac, or any good brandy
½   cup vegetable oil (safflower or grapeseed)
4   ounces sweet (unsalted) butter
2   ounces light roux, made by combining 1 ounce of melted butter with 1
    ounce of flour and cooking for 2-3 minutes

Salt, white pepper, dash of sugar

METHOD:

A. Preparing the vegetables:

Set oven at 400°. Saute shallots in 2 ounces of butter until brown. Add sugar, season lightly. Cook in the oven for 10-12 minutes, or until cooked through. Combine with the artichokes and keep warm, covered, until ready to use.

B. Preparing the chicken and the sauce:

Using a large, heavy-bottomed skillet, saute the chicken pieces, skin side down, at a high temperature, in the vegetable oil.
          When brown, turn the pieces over, reduce the heat to medium, and cook 7-8 minutes, or until done. Transfer the chicken to a platter and keep warm, covered. Dispose of the excess fat from the skillet and deglaze with the brandy, add the stock and the white wine. Reduce to 2 cups. Thicken the reduction with the roux. Add the chicken pieces, correct the seasoning, simmer for 4-5 minutes.

C. Serving:

Using a slotted spoon, transfer the chicken to 4 serving plates. Whisk the remaining 2 ounces of butter into the sauce. Spoon some sauce over each chicken piece. Top with the warm, glazed shallots and artichokes. Sprinkle with some minced chives.

MAY I SUGGEST:

Wine lovers know that artichokes do not marry well with wines. In this recipe they are not abundant enough to keep you from enjoying a good Sauvignon Blanc.

Emile Labrousse

EMILE LABROUSSE
Chef de Cuisine
The Old House in Old Mo[...]

118

HOLLANDAISE CHICKEN WITH ASPARAGUS

Terry Lowry, my wife, allows me to cook whenever I want to; in fact, encourages it. So, around 6 o'clock every evening I wander into the kitchen, pour a glass of wine, and ponder "What to create tonight?"

This dish was one of those quick, last minute decisions based on hunger, available food, and a tight schedule. I was so delighted with it that I mentioned it to Jerry Devecchio, Food Editor at Sunset Magazine. She included it in the magazine's "Chefs of the West" feature a couple of months later.

INGREDIENTS

6	chicken thighs (about 1 3/4 lbs.), skinned
2	tablespoons butter or margarine
2	tablespoons brandy
1/2	teaspoon dry basil
1	can (6 oz.) hollandaise sauce
3/4	pound asparagus, tough ends removed
1	jar (6 oz.) marinated artichokes, drained
	Chopped parsley
	Lemon wedges

Rinse chicken and pat dry. Arrange thighs in a single layer in a 7 by 11 inch glass or ceramic baking dish, dot with butter or margarine, then sprinkle with brandy and basil. Cover with plastic wrap and cook in a microwave oven on full power for 8 minutes. After 4 minutes, rotate the dish a half turn if you don't have a turntable in your microwave.

Spoon hollandaise into a small bowl; drain cooking juices from chicken into sauce and blend well with a wire whip. Push chicken pieces to opposite sides of the dish and lay asparagus in the center, with tips in the middle and stems touching both ends of the dish. Tuck artichokes around the chicken. Spoon sauce evenly over all.

Cover with plastic wrap and cook on full power until asparagus is tender when pierced, 10 to 12 minutes. Rotate dish several times. Let stand 5 minutes. Sprinkle with parsley to serve. Offer lemon wedges to squeeze over individual portions. Makes 2 or 3 servings.

Enjoy!

Fred LaCosse

Fred LaCosse / P.O. Box 31276 San Francisco, CA 94131 (415) 821-1177

CYB

ANNE LAMOTT, Novelist

(I do not have any personalized stationery, nor do I know what the initials CYB stand for, but it is currently the only paper in the house, and I have reams and reams of it, if any of you need some. How or where did I get it? Well. It is sort of a long story.)

DR. MORRIS FISHBACK'S GOOD DIP

1 pint sour cream

1 cup mayonnaise

1 bunch scallions, minced (use the gren part, too)

1 can water chestnuts, chopped up

1 package frozen spinach, thawed, with all the water squeezed out, and then chopped

1 package Knorr's dry vegetable soup mix

Combine all ingredients in a bowl, and chill for an hour, or overnight (Oh oh. This is starting to sound like those recipes first graders write up for their teachers, for things like spaghetti--"Make spaghetti sauce and then put it on noodles and put grated cheese on it too and then have it." What I meant was, chill it for at least an hour, but you can also make it a day ahead and let it chill overnight, if that is more convenient for you.)

You can serve it in a really pretty bowl, surrounded with dip chips, dip vegetables, or baguette slices--but xx if you want to get really festive, hollow out a loaf of round sourdough, and use this as the serving bowl.

> Long and happy dancing,
> and sorry about all the typos,
>
> Anne Lamott

RUTH ASAWA LANIER, INC.
1116 CASTRO STREET
SAN FRANCISCO, CALIFORNIA 94114
TEL. 415/282-9277 · 285-7639

TOFU SNACK

One package regular tofu (soybean cake)
¼ cup light, low-sodium miso (soy bean paste)
¼ cup salad oil
One Tbs. Mirin (Japanese cooking sauce) optional
Black pepper to taste (cayenne pepper for spicier taste)
2 Tbs. chopped cilantro or parsley
2 Tbs. chopped green onions
Mix miso, salad oil, mirin, and pepper in a bowl.

Rinse tofu and place on paper towel to absorb excess moisture.
Slice ½" thick vertically

Use pyrex baking dish. Brush with salad oil.
Place tofu slices in dish, and brush with ½ of miso mix.
Place under broiler. Bake for 5-7 minutes or until brown.
Turn over with spatula, brush with remaining miso mix, and
broil until brown.
Serve hot.
Garnish with chopped cilantro or parsley and chopped green onions.

Ruth Asawa Lanier
Ruth Asawa Lanier

This is a childhood snack our Mother made for us.

WILLIAMS-SONOMA

100 North Point Street
San Francisco, CA 94133
415/421-7900
Telex: 6713712 Cuisine

W. Howard Lester
President

PORC BRAISE AU WHISKEY

3 pounds pork loin in one piece, boned and tied
18 prunes
1½ to 2 cups, or more, beef bouillon
½ pound smoked ham, cut in thick slices
½ cup Dijon mustard
2/3 cup dark brown sugar
2 T's peanut oil
2/3 cup bourbon whiskey
Salt
Black pepper, freshly ground
Bouquet garni of thyme, sage and parsley

Preheat oven to 375°. Steep prunes in 1 cup warm bouillon.
Cut ham into strips, poke ham into meat with a thin, sharp
knife. Paint meat with mustard, then roll it in brown sugar.
In a heavy ovenproof iron casserole brown meat evenly in peanut oil (10 to 15 minutes). The sugar will caramelize; watch
carefully to see that it does not burn. Pour half the whiskey
over the meat and flame it. Add ½ cup of the remaining bouillon.
Cook covered in oven for 1 3/4 hours. Halfway through, turn the
meat, season with salt and pepper, add bouquet garni, and lower
to 350°. Add the prunes 10 minutes before cooking is completed.
Remove the meat to a warm platter. Remove fat, bring sauce to
a boil, adding remaining whiskey and stir to dislodge the sedi-
ments. To thicken, bring to a boil with arrowroot or cornstarch
mixed with a little cold stock or water. Season to taste.
Decorate with prune sauce and watercress.

This is a long-time favorite that we have
enjoyed often.

Ludmila Lopukhova

BLINIS (BLINTZES) WITH CABBAGE OR CHEESE

Blinis are one of Russia's most versatile dishes. They can be served with caviar as an appetizer, with a cabbage filling as a main course, or with cheese filling and jam as a dessert. In all cases sour cream is a must. My favorite is the "tvorog" cheese filling topped with homemade strawberry jam. Take care. This was the dish that persuaded my husband to marry me.

Blini Ingredients (4 blinis)
1 Egg
1 cup white flour
1 cup low fat milk
1 tablespoon sunflower oil
1/4 teaspoon salt
1/2 teaspoon sugar

Instructions
- Beat the egg in a bowl
- Add the flour and milk a little bit at a time while mixing
- Each time make sure the flour is mixed in well before adding more milk
- Add the rest of the ingredients and mix

Frying the blinis
- Use a large frying pan, very high heat
- When the pan is hot add a little bit of oil
- Use a soup ladle to pour the mix into the pan and spread it around thinly
- After the pancake is cooked on both sides put the blini on a plate

Cabbage Filling
1/2 medium sized cabbage
1/2 onion
1 Hard boiled egg
3 tablespoons oil (or butter)

Instructions
- Chop the cabbage and onion into small pieces
- Fry in a pan 15-20 minutes with butter or vegetable oil
- Chop the egg and mix with the cabbage and onion
- Roll the mixture inside the blini
- Serve with sour cream

"Tvorog" Cheese Filling
3/4 lb Farmer cheese
1 Egg
1 teaspoon sugar
1/8 teaspoon salt

Instructions
- Mix in a bowl and roll the mixture inside the blini
- Put the blintz back in the pan on low heat to warm the filling (8-10 minutes)
- Put 1 teaspoon of butter in the pan and cover
- Serve with sour cream and jam

Ludmila Lopukhova

MRS. JOHN WARD MAILLIARD III
2740 Green Street
San Francisco 94123
(415) 921-0345

TEX'S CHICKEN

"Winging it " with Charlotte "Tex" Mailliard

2 chickens - room temperature; marinade for two hours
with chopped garlic.

season chicken with salt and pepper.

Dip in buttermilk seasoned with garlic juice,
one egg, salt & pepper & cayenne.

Roll in unbleached white flour seasoned with
nutmeg, cayenne, cinnamon & cumin.

Fry in a combination of ½ Wesson oil, ¼ corn
oil and ¼ peanut oil at 340 degrees. Do dark
meat first.

SACRAMENTO ADDRESS
ROOM 4062
STATE CAPITOL
95814
PHONE (916) 445-1412

SAN FRANCISCO ADDRESS
2045 STATE BUILDING
350 MCALLISTER STREET
94102
PHONE: (415) 557-1437

MARIN ADDRESS
30 N. SAN PEDRO ROAD
SUITE 160
SAN RAFAEL, CA 94903
PHONE: (415) 479-6612

STANDING COMMITTEES
HOUSING AND URBAN AFFAIRS
(VICE CHAIRMAN)
BUDGET AND FISCAL REVIEW
JUDICIARY
LOCAL GOVERNMENT
NATURAL RESOURCES AND WILDLIFE

SUBCOMMITTEES
RIGHTS OF THE DISABLED (CHAIRMAN)
INFRASTRUCTURE AND PUBLIC WORKS
(CHAIRMAN)
ADMINISTRATION OF JUSTICE
OFFSHORE OIL AND GAS DEVELOPMENT

SELECT COMMITTEES
MARITIME INDUSTRY (CHAIRMAN)
CITIZEN PARTICIPATION IN GOVERNMENT
PACIFIC RIM
VICTIMS' RIGHTS

JOINT COMMITTEES
FISHERIES AND AQUACULTURE
STATE'S ECONOMY
LEGISLATIVE BUDGET COMMITTEE

COMMISSIONS
CALIFORNIA STATE GOVERNMENT
ORGANIZATION AND ECONOMY
STATUS OF WOMEN

SENATOR
MILTON MARKS
THIRD SENATORIAL DISTRICT

REPRESENTING

SAN FRANCISCO - MARIN

IN THE

𝔖enate

CHAIRMAN

𝔖enate 𝔐ajority 𝔠aucus

OX TAILS

Three (3) Oxtails disjointed

soak in cold water

drain and dry

brown in butter

add one can of stewed tomatoes

three (3) cups of consomme

1/2 cup of uncooked barley

one (1) bunch of carrots--cut

bay leaves--several

six (6) whole peppers

Cover and put in 350 degree oven--cook for 4 hours; separate fat from juice and take off fat. Combine and heat. Wine may be added if desired.

This was one of my mother's favorite recipes and mine, too.

Milton Marks

Mary Martin

COLONIAL CHICKEN

One frying chicken, one and one-half cups
sifted all-purpose flour, one and one-half
teaspoons baking powder, teaspoon salt, four
eggs, one and one-half cups milk, three
tablespoons melted butter, black pepper.

Cut chicken into serving size pieces, reserving
back and neck for stock. Roll pieces in flour,
seasoned with salt and pepper. Brown all sides
in one-fourth inch shortening in frying pan.
Remove. Drain while batter being prepared.

Batter: Sift flour, baking powder, salt
into bowl. Beat eggs in second bowl until
light. Stir in milk and melted butter. Blend
egg mixture into dry ingredients; beat until
batter is smooth. Pour batter into buttered
baking dish; arrange browned chicken on top
of batter, sprinkle with black pepper. Bake
in moderate oven, 350 degrees F. one hour,
or until batter is puffed and golden brown.

Serve at once with Cream Giblet Gravy.

Six servings.

_Love,
Mary —_

Friends OF THE SAN FRANCISCO PUBLIC Library

Main Library ⌒ Civic Center, San Francisco, California 94102 ⌒ 415-558-3857

MARGARET MAYER, EXECUTIVE DIRECTOR

Fresh Fruits in Ginger Sauce

serves 6-8

1   small pineapple
1/2 pound seedless green grapes
1   pint strawberries
2   tablespoons sugar
1   cup fresh orange juice
1/3 cup sugar
1   tablespoon lemon juice
2   tablespoons dark rum
1   tablespoon minced crystallized ginger

Peel, quarter, and core pineapple. Cut each quarter in half lengthwise.
Cut into very thin fan-shaped slices. Slice the grapes in half and add
to pineapple. Gently rinse berries, remove hulls and slice in half.
Put berries in a small separate bowl, sprinkle with 2 tablespoons of
sugar and chill.   In a small pan, mix orange juice with 1/3 cup sugar
and lemon juice. Bring to a boil, lower the heat and simmer for 20
minutes. Remove from heat; stir in rum and ginger. Add sauce to
pineapple and grapes. Chill. Add strawberries and their juice just
before serving.

Margaret Mayer, Friend of Books, Fine Food, and the Ballet

ANCHOR BREWING CO.

1705 MARIPOSA STREET SAN FRANCISCO CALIFORNIA 94107 TELEPHONE 415·863·8350

I have encountered many "beer recipes" over the years because I have long been interested in cooking with beer. The following is my all-time favorite. One night not long ago my friend Angel Stoyanof hosted a unique dinner, with many dishes all including one of Anchor's beers as an ingredient. It was a joint effort of Stoyanof's Restaurant in Corte Madera and Monterey Fish Company of Berkeley.

Everyone's favorite was the following sorbet developed by David Stevenson of Stoyanof's. We loved it for its own sake, the sorbet is exquisite. But also because it captured the unique, subtle character of our Wheat Beer and integrated it so successfully into a surprising dish. I think it is terrific.

ANCHOR WHEAT BEER SORBET

1 1/2 cups sugar
2/3 cup water
1/4 cup lime juice

1/4 cup lemon juice
2 1/2 cups Anchor Wheat Beer
1/8 tsp. salt

Combine water and sugar in a sauce pan. Bring to a boil over medium heat, stirring constantly. Reduce heat and gently simmer for 5 minutes. Remove from heat and allow mixture to cool. When cool, combine syrup with remaining ingredients, mixing well. Freeze as directed using an ice cream maker.

If an ice cream maker is not available, place the ingredients in a chilled stainless steel or ceramic bowl. Place in freezer. As the mixture begins to freeze, 30 minutes or so, remove from freezer and whisk so as to combine frozen portions along the surface and the side of the bowl with the non-frozen portions. Repeat this process every 30 minutes until a very thick slush is obtained. Allow this mixture to freeze overnight.

Fritz Maytag

JESSICA M^cCLINTOCK INC.

CRETONS

*** Ingredients ***

1 lb. pork loin chops (ideally 3 parts meat to 1 part fat)
1½ medium onions, minced
1 cup milk (or amount sufficient to cover meat)
¼ teaspoon <u>each</u> of salt, pepper & ground clove (or to taste)

*** Prepare pork ***

Cut all meat off bones, keeping all fat.
Cut meat into small (1-1½") cubes.

*** To Cook ***

Combine cubed meat and minced onion in heavy saucepan. Cover with milk
and cook uncovered over medium heat for at least 1 hour, stirring often,
until meat is mashable with a fork. Cool completely. Mash with fork
(for chunky texture) or puree in food processor (for smooth texture)
with all cooking liquids and fats.

Check seasoning and adjust if needed. If you wish, transfer to a
pretty china crock or other container. Chill thoroughly.

*** To Serve ***

Mornings I would wake up to the aroma of cretons, one of my favorite
foods which my grandmother would prepare and then serve on hot, buttered
buckwheat pancakes rolled up. (May also be served on crackers, if you
like.)

Most of my formative years were spent in a very small village in
northern Maine called Frenchville. This quaint village is located only
a few miles from the Canadian border and the area is known as French
Acadian. This is where French Acadian cuisine originated. The area is
primarily farmland and with such a bounty of fresh pork and chicken we
enjoyed many meals such as cretons.

Having left northern Maine to live in Boston and now in California, I
have recently rediscovered this recipe which my father gave to me and
which I now pass on to you.

Jessica McClintock

1400 SIXTEENTH STREET, SAN FRANCISCO, CALIFORNIA 94103 415.495.3030

SAN FRANCISCO OPERA

WAR MEMORIAL OPERA HOUSE • SAN FRANCISCO, CALIFORNIA 94102

TERENCE A. McEWEN
General Director

SIR JOHN PRITCHARD
Music Director

3 November 1986

Mr. George B. James, President
SF Ballet Board of Trustees
S. Bronfman II, President
The Seagram Classics Wine Co.
Ingrid Weiss, President
SF Ballet Auxiliary
Mrs. Edward Plant
Chairman, San Francisco Celebrity Chefs
650 California Street
San Francisco, California 94108

Dear Committee:

I am writing in response to your letter requesting a recipe from me
for your cookbook. Unfortunately, my finest hour in the kitchen has
to do with a perfect soft-boiled egg. That's about my limit, other
than a tuna-fish sandwich or an English muffin.

(The glamorous life of an opera director)

I wish you all the very best with your project; I'm sure it will be a
great success, without, regretfully, my participation.

Kindest regards,

Terence A. McEwen

TAM:ml

. . . . mumble, mumble, mumble UH-OH, late turning
in that recipe for the San Francisco Celebrity
Chefs Cookbook, my one shot at immortality. (If
they only knew the kind of cooking that gets done
around my house these days, the sandwiches sand-
wiched in between newspaper column deadlines . . .
is there such a thing as a "celebrity short
order cook"?) Oh, well. What they don't know
won't hurt them, and neither will my former mother-
in-law's Rum Pudding. Sure, it's an artery-clogger,
but it's delicious, and where food's concerned,
that counts for a lot. At least it does with me.
Who wants to wind up a great meal xxkhxAixxMxxxxxxx
xxxxxRxxkxkxxxx with something sensible, like a
carrot stick?

Where's that letter they sent me? It's there
under the rubble somewhere, I know. I think they
wanted this thing on my personal stationery, but
since I don't have any, maybe a clean piece of
paper will do. Anything nasty stuck to this one?
Nope. Looks okay. Now if my typewriter weren't
dying of metal fatigue, and I'm out of stamps again,
and that evil red light on the answering machine
keeps blinking away, and somebody's at the front
door . . .

mumble, mumble, mumble LET'S GET ON WITH IT:

Ingrid McFadden's Rum Pudding

Beat until lemon-colored:

        8 egg yolks
        1 Cup sugar

Bring
~~BRING~~
~~xxxxx~~ to a boil, stirring:

        1 quart cream
        2 envelopes plain gelatin

When cool, blend with the yolks and sugar. Add 1/2 Cup
Meyer's dark rum. Pour into wet molds, the small
metal kind with fluted rims, or one decorative ring
mold. Chill for several hours or overnight, unmold
and serve with thin cookies. No sauces, though, because the rum has an assertive flavor.

The texture's best if you use half whipping cream and
half half 'n half. (There must be a better way of
putting that.)

Recipe can be halved and is quick and idiot-proof.

HOT ARTICHOKE HEART DIP

Two 14-ounce cans Artichoke Hearts
   (not the marinated kind)
      drain and chop
1 cup Parmesan Cheese
1 cup shredded Mozzarella Cheese
1 cup Mayonnaise
1 teaspoon Salt
1 minced Garlic Clove

Preheat oven to 350°. Butter a souffle' dish.

Mix all ingredients thoroughly in a large bowl. Spoon mixture into prepared dish. Bake for 25 to 30 minutes. Serve hot with melba toast. Serves 10.

Herbert McLaughlin

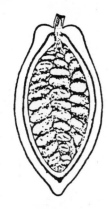

MARQUISE AU CHOCOLAT   (Alice Medrich/Cocolat)

4 cup heart-shaped (or other) mold
10 oz bittersweet or semi-sweet chocolate, cut into small pieces
4 oz sweet butter, cut into pieces
4 large eggs, separated
1/8 tsp cream of tartar
2 T sugar
2 tsp powdered instant coffee dissolved in 1 tsp water (optional)
2 T cocoa powder

Combine chocolate and butter in a bowl set in a barely simmering water bath. Stir to hasten melting. When melted and smooth whisk in egg yolks and coffee flavoring if desired. Set aside.

In a clean dry mixer bowl combine egg whites and cream of tartar. Whip until soft peaks form then sprinkle in sugar and whip until stiff but not dry. Fold 1/4 to 1/3 of meringue into chocolate mixture to lighten it, then fold remaining meringue into chocolate and turn immediately into prepared mold. Chill several hours before unmolding to serve.

To serve dip pan in hot water, wipe dry and reverse onto a serving platter. Dust Marquise with cocoa by sifting it gently through a small fine strainer. Serve thin slices with Creme Anglaise or Fresh Cream Dessert Sauce.

Alice Medrich

Retail Locations: Berkeley • Oakland • San Francisco • Palo Alto

GARDNER AND LANI MEIN
request the pleasure of
your company

MENU

Oyster, Mushroom Soup
Seahorse Salad*
Bagelsticks/Goat Cheese
Fruit
Cookies/Lemon Sorbet/Coffee

Seahorse Salad*

2 bunches spinach (washed, leaves only)
1 bunch chicory (washed, leaves only)
1 red-leaf lettuce (washed, leaves only)
1 can hearts of palm cut in $\frac{1}{4}$" lengths
2 lbs. smoked New Zealand mussels
$\frac{1}{4}$ lb. feta cheese crumbled
oil, vinegar, Italian herbs
Chinese angel-hair noodles tinted green

Combine all and toss with Italian dressing
of your choice. Place on plate or buffet
platter with a surround of green angel-hair
noodles (like delicate seaweed). Serves 12.

Rum Doo Doos

$2\frac{1}{4}$ ozs. St. James Rum
$1\frac{1}{4}$ ozs. Meyers Rum
2 fresh oranges
1 peach
1 lime
3 strawberries
sprig of mint

Shake by hand. Add ice and
one long stick of watermelon.
Serve in stem wine glass.

DEADPAN POSSUM
or
THE PIANIST PLAYS POSSUM

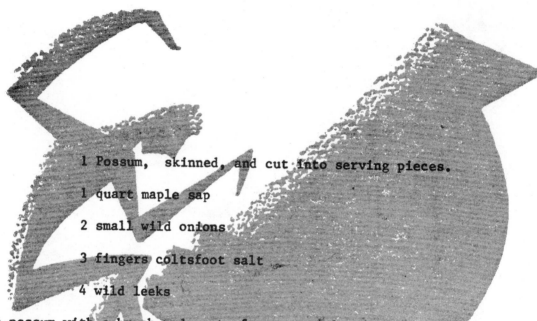

1 Possum, skinned, and cut into serving pieces.

1 quart maple sap

2 small wild onions

3 fingers coltsfoot salt

4 wild leeks

Clean possum with a brush made out of evergreen boughs.
Pour sap into a birch bark container (or other non-metallic container).
Cut up the onions into pieces and add to the sap.
Layer possum meat, leeks, and salt in the solution. Let stand
overnight in a cool place.

In the morning, grease the stone griddle with fat, remove meat
from the marinade and fry on the griddle. Serve with hot cornmeal cakes.

Nearly impossible to find in every-day type meat stores, Frank Onorato
& Company (1540 Fillmore Street, San Francisco) sells possum for only
three weeks a year, during the month of December.

Fat and tender, a possum can taste almost like a suckling pig!

Peter Mintun

6411 Regent Street
Oakland
California 94618

I am honored to be asked to send a recipe for your
cookbook. This is actually the second time I have had
such a request -- and may, I fear, be the last.

To explain: Circa 30 years ago, when my son Benjamin
Treuhaft was a dear little tot of 7 or thereabouts, the
local PTA was preparing a cook book consisting of the
favorite recipes of the children's mothers. So Benj came
dashing in one day, saying "What's your favorite food?
And how do you cook it?" "Roast duck," I answered. "But
how do you cook it?" "Well, you get a duck, put it in the
oven and roast until done." "What would you have with it?"
"Green salad." "How do you make that?" "You get some
lettuce and put dressing on."

Sad to say, that's exactly how the recipe appeared in
the PTA cookery book. "Jessica Mitford's Duck Dinner:
Put a duck in the oven and cook until done. Green Salad:
Put dressing on lettuce." Needless to say, all the other
moms had myriad delicious ingredients for complex things
like brownies. I was abashed.

But thinking it over, mine will I believe withstand
the test of time, if followed closely, exactly as given
in the PTA cookbook.

Jessica Mitford

Jessica Mitford

FRANCES MOFFAT

311 Union Street • San Francisco, CA 94133
(415) 362-8851

NORTH BEACH SPECIAL

A rich, hearty casserole version of a favorite San Franciso dish.

2 lbs. lean ground beef
2 pkgs. frozen chopped spinach
1/2 lb. fresh sliced mushrooms
1 egg, beaten
1 onion, thinly sliced

2 tbsps. oil or margarine
3/4 c. sour cream
1 c. grated Romano cheese
3/4 c. grated Gruyere cheese
salt, oregano, basil to taste

Brown onion in oil or margarine. Add meat, saute until brown; add mushrooms and barely cook. Set aside. Cook spinach and squeeze out moisture, then add to meat and mushrooms. Mix in egg, sour cream, 1/2 Romano cheese, all Gruyere cheese. Season with salt, oregano and basil. Mix thoroughly and turn into large casserole. Top with remaining Romano cheese. Bake in 375 degree oven until thoroughly hot and top cheese melts.

Serves 6.

JOHN L. MOLINARI
President, Board of Supervisors
Room 235, City Hall
San Francisco, California 94102

MOLINARI'S FAVORITE CHICKEN

4 chicken breasts, boned and halved
1/2 cup flour
4 slices of prosciutto (Italian ham)
3 tbs. olive oil
3 tbs. unsalted butter
1/2 cup sauterne
dashes of pepper, oregano, sweet basil, tarragon and
paprika
1 cup sauteed mushrooms

Dredge chicken in flour and season with pepper. Roll each
chicken breast and wrap with one slice of prosciutto.
Secure with a toothpick.

Heat olive oil and butter in heavy skillet and add
sauterne. Place chicken in skillet and sprinkle with
herbs. Cover and cook until tender.

Sprinkle with paprika for color. Top with sauteed
mushrooms. Serve with artichoke hearts and wild rice.

Enjoy!

On behalf of both myself and my wife, Louise, we thank you
for the opportunity to participate in the San Francisco
Ballet's Celebrity Chef Cookbook. Bon appetit and our
best wishes for a successful 1987 season.

PAT MONTANDON

Vitello Tonnato

Remove the skin and fat from a 2 pound boned leg of veal. Make several incisions in the meat, and insert an anchovy filet in each. Roll up the meat and tie it with string. Put the meat in a large kettle and cover with boiling water in which you have placed 1 onion stuck with 4 cloves, 2 bay leafs, 2 stalks celery with leafs, 1 carrot quartered, a few sprigs parsley, and a little salt and pepper. Cover and simmer for 1½ hours. Remove meat from broth and let it cool thoroughly.

In food processor with blade, place 1½ cups tuna (packed in oil), 6 anchovy filets, and 1 generous cup olive oil and blend to make a light paste. Thin the sauce with the juice of 2 lemons and stir in ½ cup drained small capers. The sauce should be very smooth and quite thick.

Slice the cold meat very thin and arrange the slices in a shallow terrine; pour the sauce around them. Marinate over night in refrigerator. Serve in the terrine garnished with rolled anchovies stuffed with capers.

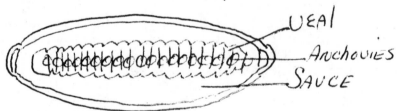

VEAL
Anchovies
Sauce

Great to do ahead for buffet suppers! Very Italian. It is always a favorite of people who come to my Roundtable Luncheons!

Washington Square
Bar & Grill.

1707 Powell St. San Francisco, 94133 Ph. 982-8123

This seems to be the year of Polenta. Everyone is discovering
this healthy golden grain, and devising delicious ways to serve it.
Here are two of our favorites:

Polenta with Poached Egg and Tomato Sauce: (serves four)
    2 cups San Marzano Tomatoes and their puree, processed briefly
    7 cloves of garlic, minced
    ½ onion, chopped fine
    2 TBSP.Italian parsley or Basil, chopped
    1 TBSP Extra Virgin Olive Oil

Combine 1st 3 ingredients in non-reactive pan and cook over moderately
high flame 20 minutes. Stir in the herbs and oil.
Poach 4 eggs in the tomato sauce, and serve one egg and some sauce
atop four bowls of soft-stirred polenta (recipe below).

Polenta with Sausage Sauce: (serves four)

    2 Italian sausages, sweet or hot, crumbled in a saucepan
    2 oz. pancetta bacon, chopped
Cook the sausage and pancetta together, adding a tsp. olive oil if
needed, till sausage loses its pink color. Add the above tomato
sauce and cook another 10 minutes. Serve atop four bowls of soft-
stirred polenta (recipe follows).

Soft-stirred Polenta: (serves four)

    1 cup coarse polenta
    3 cups chicken broth (or water and salt)
Bring liquid to boil and slowly stir in the polenta. Cook, stirring,
a minimum of 20 minutes, adding more liquid (or butter) as needed to
keep polenta from drying out.

NOTE: The Italian way with polenta is to cook it slowly as long
as possible, to allow it to develop a nutty flavor. Addicts can
get an electric polenta pan that stirs it for you throughout the
hour it takes to develop that deep, nutty taste..

Mary Etta Moose

3000 SAND HILL ROAD

MENLO PARK, CALIFORNIA 94025

(415) 854-1040

MAILING ADDRESS: ·

POST OFFICE BOX 7657

MENLO PARK, CALIFORNIA 94025

MERVIN G. MORRIS
PRESIDENT

POULET GRILLE

(Serves 8)

2 3-3 1/2 lb. chickens - backbones removed.

In a small bowl combine - 1/2 cup Dijon Mustard
                          1/4 tsp. cayenne pepper
                          4 tbsp. fine chopped shallots

                  Set aside.

Preheat oven to 450 degrees. Dry chicken and season with salt and pepper.
Place skin side up in a roasting pan. Pour over chicken - 6 tbsp. melted
butter. Bake for 25-30 minutes - baste occasionally. Remove from oven.
Paint with mustard mixture and sprinkle with fresh bread crumbs - 1/2 cup
crumbs per chicken. Finish cooking under broiler - 5 to 10 minutes.

MGM:mrf
11/6/86

140

Gina Moscone

TUSCAN WHITE BEAN SOUP

½ pound Large Great Northern White Beans
2-3 bay leaves
Basil
3 tablespoons good olive oil
¼ cup parsley, finely chopped
3 cloves of garlic, finely chopped
juice of 1 lemon

Soak beans overnight. Drain. Cover with 2 quarts
of water in a pot, preferably ceramic. Add bay leaves
and basil and 3T olive oil. Let simmer for 2 hours.
Add 2T salt and cook another 30 minutes. Sieve
½ the beans or use food processor. Mix puree with
rest of beans. Add parsley and garlic. Before serving,
stir ¼ to ½ cups of good olive oil, lemon juice and,
if needed, added salt. Reheat. Serve over coarse
bread rubbed with garlic, salt and sprinkled with
olive oil.

I first tasted this soup after a hectic day of
Christmas shopping. Having pushed my way through crowds
for most of the day, I came home tired, grumpy, and
the last thing I wanted to do was cook. To my surprise,
my daughter Jenifer had prepared this soup for me. It
was so delicious that every holiday season, I make sure
there's enough white bean soup to last until the
Christmas tree is taken down. I'm glad I can share this
recipe with you. Buon Appetito!

Gina Moscone

STANLEY MOSK, JUSTICE

Sicilian Cassata
12 servings

5 peeled orange slices
2 cups heavy cream
1 1/3 cups (about 12 oz.) whole milk ricotta cheese
3 tablespoons plus 2 teaspoons sugar
4 tablespoons (about 2 oz.) finely chopped candied orange peel or citron
3 tablespoons (*6 tablespoons) coarsely chopped semisweet chocolate
1 teaspoon finely grated orange zest
1/4 cup plus 1 teaspoon orange liqueur
1 pound cake 9" x 31/2"

*   If you love chocolate as much as I do, use the larger amount in parentheses.

1. Beat 1/2 cup of the cream until soft peaks form. In a medium bowl, mix the ricotta and 3 tablespoons of the sugar. Fold in the whipped cream, 3 tablespoons of the citron, the chocolate, orange zest and 1/4 cup of the liqueur.

2. Cut the cake crosswise into 3/8-inch slices. Line the bottom and sides of a 1 1/2 quart bowl with a layer of cake slices, trimming or shaping as necessary.

3. Spoon a layer of the ricotta filling about 3/4-inch deep over the bottom. Cover with a layer of cake slices. Repeat with two more layers of filling and cake, trimming the cake slices as necessary. Press gently to level the top slices with the sides, cover and refrigerate for 4 hours, or preferably overnight.

4. To unmold, invert cake onto a platter. (To facilitate easier unmolding first butter sides of bowl and line with waxed paper before making cake. Then to unmold soak towel in hot water and drape over bowl until cake easily slips out.)

5. Beat the remaining 1 1/2 cups cream, 2 teaspoons sugar and 1 teaspoon liqueur until stiff peaks form. Cover the cake with the whipped cream using knife to make small peaks in decorative fashion. Pinwheel the orange slices on top, dribble remaining chocolate over them and stud the sides with the remaining citron. May be refrigerated several hours before serving.

It looks so beautiful and tastes so unusual everyone will swear it came from the newest "in" bakery. Guests at our home have raved about it.

Stanley Mosk

142

PIERRE
AT MERIDIEN

OYSTERS IN CHAMPAGNE

INGREDIENTS FOR 4 PERSONS:

- 24 OYSTERS
- 2 SHALLOTS
- ½ POUND OF UNSALTED BUTTER
- 1 CUP OF (GOOD) CHAMPAGNE
- 1 MEDIUM LEEK
- 1 MEDIUM CELERY RIB
- 1 MEDIUM CARROT
- 1 SPRIG PARSLEY
- SALT AND PEPPER TO TASTE
- ROCK SALT

Wash and arrange the oysters on a tray. Put in a hot oven until they open.
Finely dice two shallots and simmer them until soft in a sauce pan with a
little butter.   Add the champagne and, half way through the reduction, the
strained oyster juices.

Whisk in the butter bit by bit over low heat, and strain. Cut the vegetables
in a fine julienne; blanch in salty water and drain.

In a soup plate, arrange the oyster shells, place the vegetable julienne first,
the oysters and back in the oven for two minutes so it is hot.
Before serving pour the champagne butter over with a leaf of Italian parsley.

To be served with champagne, of course !

> The last thing to ask a chef is to cook on his day off, but
> cooking with champagne is always a pleasure to me.
> The test starts in your kitchen before the meal and the secret
> of this recipe is using a good champagne and above all a
> strong will not to pour all the champagne in your glass!

Santé !

Jean-Pierre Moullé

Jean-Pierre Moullé
Food & Beverage Director

50 Third Street, San Francisco, CA 94103, Tel. (415) 974-6400

TURK MURPHY JAZZ BAND
of San Francisco

CRISP TOFFEE BARS

1 cup margarine
1 cup brown sugar
1 tsp. vanilla extract

----

2 cups sifted flour
1 - 6oz Package semi-sweet chocolate pieces
1 cup chopped walnuts

Thoroughly cream together butter , sugar and vanilla. Add flour and mix well.
Stir in chocolate and walnuts.
Press mixture into ungreased 15½ by 10½ jellyroll pan one inch deep. (Any pan
of similiar dimensions may be substituted).

Bake at 350 degrees for 25 minutes or until browned.

While warm, cut into bars or squares. Cool before removing from pan.
This should make about five dozen pieces which are delicious and the method
is fast, easy and simple.

Turk Murphy

I had no idea this heavenly dish was from Sunset. I always assumed that it was born in my grandmother's kitchen, whence it became known simply as "Nana's Lemon Pie," now carried on by my mother in her grand tradition. Culinary angels, both of them.

Gerald Nachman

Angel Pie

Angel Pie immediately became a favorite when the recipe first appeared in *Sunset Magazine* several decades ago.

    4 eggs, separated
    ½ teaspoon cream of tartar
      Pinch of salt
    1½ cups sugar
      Grated peel of 2 lemons
    3 tablespoons lemon juice
    1 cup (½ pt.) whipping cream

Beat egg whites until frothy, sprinkle in cream of tartar and salt, and beat until stiff. Beat in 1 cup of the sugar, 2 tablespoons at a time. The mixture should be glossy and stand in stiff peaks when all the sugar has been added.

With the back of a tablespoon, spread meringue in a well-greased 9-inch pie pan, pushing it high on the sides so that it resembles a pie shell. Bake in a 300° oven for 40 minutes. Cool on a rack.

Beat egg yolks and the remaining ½ cup sugar in the top of a double boiler until light. Stir in lemon peel and juice and cook over hot water until thick, stirring constantly. Chill. Whip cream and fold into chilled lemon mixture. Fill meringue shell with lemon filling; chill for several hours. Serves 6 to 8.

EXECUTIVE OFFICES

Through the sixties I enjoyed exercising in my professional hotel career for nearly nine years in the city of New Orleans. This simple recipe of merely eight ingredients brings back memories of untold joy and pleasure. I remember the crisp, crusty French style New Orleans bread which was so delicious dipped in the melted butter and lemon and rosemary of this dish. Do not under any circumstance remove the peel from the shrimp until they are cooked. It is from the shells the pleasure which I describe is derived in terms of flavor!

NEW ORLEANS STYLE
ROSEMARY-LEMON-BUTTER SHRIMP

INGREDIENTS:

- 1½ lb. butter
- 6   oz. Worcestershire
- 8   Tb. black pepper
- 1   tsp ground rosemary
- 4   lemons, sliced
- 1   tsp Tabasco
- 4   tsp salt
- 8-10 lb. shrimp

PROCEDURE:

Melt butter in a saucepan. Add Worcestershire, pepper, rosemary, lemon slices, Tabasco, salt and mix thoroughly. Divide shrimp between two large shallow pans and pour heated sauce over each. Stir well. Cook at 400 degrees for 12-15 minutes. Shells will turn pink when cooked.

Good eatin',

James A. Nassikas
President and Managing Partner

APRICOT OMELETTE LAYER

1/2 cup butter
1 cup flour
1-1/4 cups cream
3/4 cup milk
Little sugar

6 egg yolks
1 tsp. vanilla
6 egg whites

Cook milk, cream and butter together in double boiler.

Then add flour.

Stir until it leaves the sides.

Let dough cool.

Then add 6 yolks of eggs.

Beat well and add 1 tsp. vanilla.

Beat 6 whites with a little sugar until stiff and fold carefully into mixture.

Pour into 3 layer cake pans.

Bake in 325 oven 25 - 30 minutes.

Then spread hot apricot jam between layers just before serving.

Serve hot.

Pass with a bowl of whipped cream.

This is an "ooh and aah" dessert that has been served by our family for three generations.
It never fails to impress.
we never make enough!

Ellen Magnin Newman
(Mrs. Walter S.)

NEWTON

CRACKLING DUCK WITH CHESTNUT-PLUM SAUCE IN BED OF WILD RICE

Ingredients:
1 medium size duck (fresh or
    frozen)
1 whole orange
1 whole onion, peeled
8 5-star spice
1 small can of chestnut sauce
1 small can of plums
1/2 lb wild rice
1 8 oz. can chicken broth

Duck preparation:

Thaw duck at room temperature.
Wash and dry. Rub in garlic, salt
and pepper. Leave on roasting rack
for a couple of hours to dry. Stuff
duck with onion, orange and 5-star
spice. Place in a deep roasting pan
with a rack that raises the duck 3"
from bottom. Cook in pre-heated
oven at 400° for an hour. Turn
temperature down to 350° and cook
for another hour. Drain fat every
45 minutes.

Wild rice:

Cook wild rice slowly in chicken
stock in double boiler.

You can make this look very
pretty by serving the wild
rice in a tomato basket and
the chestnut-plum sauce in a
kiwi basket.

This dish is sensational
with Merlot.

Chestnut-plum sauce:

Liquify plums (after draining and
removing stone) with 1/2 can of
chestnut puree, add a few drops of
tabasco, lemon juice and a pinch
of cinnamon and nutmeg. Warm in
small sauce boat.

* * * * * *

Being Chinese, we eat only the crispy skin and the kitchen help
gets the meat. The first time I served this dish to Western
friends, they looked utterly surprised when I carved them only
the skin and sent the meat back to the kitchen. They asked, "What
was wrong with the meat?" I could not understand why they would
assume something was wrong with the meat and did not answer. I
thought they were rude; they thought I was weird!

NEWTON VINEYARD 2555 MADRONA ST. HELENA CA 94574 707 963 9000 TELEX 278732

CAMPTON PLACE
H O T E L

ROASTED EGGPLANT & TOMATO SOUP WITH SCALLION CREAM

INGREDIENTS: Serves 10

3	medium eggplants
3	Spanish yellow onions, thinly sliced
1 1/2	cans Progresso Tomatoes, 28 oz. size
8	cloves garlic
3	quarts chicken stock
4	bell peppers, green and red
	Kosher salt to taste
	black pepper, freshly cracked to taste
	olive oil

PROCEDURE:

Cut eggplant in half, lengthwise, and grill. Peel away black skin and set aside.

In a roasting pan place enough olive oil to coat the bottom and put in a 400° oven until very hot. Add onions, garlic and peppers to caramelize, stirring often. Cook for about 10 minutes. Add the roasted eggplant, tomatoes and juice and cook for another 10 minutes. Add the chicken stock and transfer to a kettle simmering for 10 minutes longer. Season to taste and puree.

To serve: strain and heat the mixture. Place in a soup bowl and garnish with 1 Tablespoon scallion cream.

SCALLION CREAM

INGREDIENTS:

1	cup sour cream
1	cup creme fraiche
1	cup scallions, thinly sliced whites and part of the greens
3	Tablespoons Sherry vinegar

PROCEDURE:

fold sour cream into creme fraiche

Trim and thoroughly wash the green ends from 3 bunches of scallions. Place in cuisinart and puree with 3 Tablespoons Sherry vinegar. Strain juice from scallion, fold into sour cream mixture, reserve for soup (discard pulp).

Let sit for at least ½ hour before using, so flavors have a chance to blend.

EXECUTIVE CHEF BRADLEY OGDEN

POLLO AI PEPERONI
Marinated Chicken with Peppers

1 chicken, about 3 pounds, or 4 whole boneless chicken breasts (boning is opptional)
2 lemons and zest from both, save for juice for marinade
10 sprigs of Italian parsley (or ½ bunch)
3/4 cup olive oil
4 bell peppers (2 red, and 2 green for presentation)
½ teaspoon oregano
1 dozen black olives
4 cloves garlic
¼ cup white wine
salt and freshly ground black pepper to taste

1. Wash chicken and cut it into 8 pieces. Place pieces in a bowl.

2. Squeeze the lemons and add the   juice and zest to the bowl
   with the chicken.

3. Mince parsley and add it to the chicken along with ½ cup of the oil.
   Sprinkle with salt and pepper. Mix everything together well and marinate
   for an hour, stirring occasionally.

4. Remove chicken from the marinade to a baking dish. Pour over the
   remaining ¼ cup oil. Preheat oven to 400 degrees and bake chicken for
   35 minutes.

5. Transfer the marinade to a saucepan.

6. Slice peppers horizontally into ½ inch rings. Place in saucepan with
   marinade and saute for about 15 minutes over medium heat. Taste for
   salt and pepper.

7. When chicken is done, place it on a warm serving dish and arrange the
   peppers and the sauce around it. Serve hot.

My good friends at Creatin Catering helped me come up with this —

B Hok

Examiner

HUNGARIAN CUCUMBER SALAD — A FAVOURITE!

```
5 OZ CUCUMBER PER PERSON
SALTED WATER
VINEGAR (WHITE)
SOUR CREAM
PAPRIKA, SALT, SUGAR.


PEEL AND WASH THE CUCUMBERS AND SLICE THEM PAPER THIN.
SOAK FOR A COUPLE OF HOURS, COVERED IN SALTED WATER.
AFTER SOAKING, SQUEEZE OUT THE WATER BY HAND.
ARRANGE ON A FLAT GLASS DISH.
MIX 3 TABLESPOONS WATER,  1 TABLESPOON VINEGAR,  PINCH
OF SUGAR,  DASH OF SALT AND 3 - 4 TABLESPOONS  SOUR CREAM.
POUR OVER CUCUMBERS AND SPRINKLE WITH PAPRIKA.

DELICIOUS WITH RICH FOOD.
```

Gladys Perint Palmer
Fashion (not food!) editor

LEON E. PANETTA
16TH DISTRICT, CALIFORNIA

COMMITTEES:
AGRICULTURE
CHAIRMAN
SUBCOMMITTEE ON DOMESTIC
MARKETING, CONSUMER RELATIONS,
AND NUTRITION

HOUSE ADMINISTRATION
CHAIRMAN
SUBCOMMITTEE ON PERSONNEL AND POLICE

SELECT COMMITTEE ON HUNGER
CHAIRMAN
TASK FORCE ON DOMESTIC HUNGER

DEPUTY MAJORITY WHIP

WASHINGTON OFFICE:
339 CANNON HOUSE OFFICE BUILDING
WASHINGTON, DC 20515
(202) 225-2861

DISTRICT OFFICES:
380 ALVARADO STREET
MONTEREY, CA 93940
(408) 649-3555

HOLLISTER, CA
(408) 637-0500

SALINAS, CA
(408) 424-2229

SAN LUIS OBISPO, CA
(805) 541-0143

SANTA CRUZ, CA
(408) 429-1976

Congress of the United States
House of Representatives
Washington, DC 20515

BASIC POTATO DUMPLINGS
Gnocchi di Patate

8 medium potatoes, preferably russets	1 tablespoon vegetable oil
1 egg yolk	¼ cup butter
1 tablespoon salt	½ cup freshly grated
2 to 2½ cups all-purpose flour	Parmesan cheese

Preheat oven to 350F (175C). With fork, puncture potatoes in several places. Bake 1 hour or until tender. Remove insides of baked potatoes; discard skins. Mash hot potatoes through a ricer or food mill into a large bowl; let cool slightly. Add egg yolk, 1 tablespoon salt and 2 cups flour; mix well. Put potato mixture on a working surface or wooden board and knead into a ball. Mixture should be soft and slightly sticky. If it is too sticky, add more flour. Lightly flour working surface and your hands. Break dough into pieces the size of large eggs. Shape pieces into rolls about the thickness of your thumb. Cut rolls into 1-inch pieces. Hold a fork with its tines resting on a work surface at a 45 degree angle and the inside curve toward you. Take a dumpling roll and press it with your index finger against the outside curve of the fork at the tip end. Quickly slide dumpling up and along the length of the tines, pressing with index finger. Remove finger and let dumpling fall back onto work surface. Grooves made by fork and finger indentation will absorb any sauce served with dumplings. Repeat with remaining dumpling rolls. Arrange dumplings on a floured tray or large plate. Fill a large saucepan two-thirds full with salted water. Bring water to a boil. Add oil and dumplings. When dumplings come to surface of water, cook 10 to 12 seconds. If dumplings remain in water any longer they will absorb water and become too soft. Remove dumplings with a slotted spoon or strainer, draining against side of saucepan. Place in a warm dish. Serve hot with butter and Parmesan cheese or your favorite sauce. Makes 8 servings.

Variation:

Potatoes can be boiled instead of baked. Do not puncture potatoes before cooking or they will absorb water, making it necessary to add extra flour to dumpling mixture.

This is one of my favorite recipes:

Turkey Chardonnay

Ingredients

1 pound sliced Turkey breast	1/2 cup of butter
4 tablespoons parmesean cheese	1/4 pound of mushrooms
2 tablespoons flour	3 tablespoons chopped onion
1 teaspoon salt	3/4 cup of Pat Paulsen Chardonnay
1/4 teaspoon white pepper	1 chicken boullion cube
1/4 teaspoon garlic salt	2 tablespoons snipped parsley

Directions:

Mix the cheese, flour, and seasoning and coat the Turkey breast slices.

Melt 1/4 cup butter in skillet over medium heat.

Saute slices until golden brown about 3 min. on each side.

Remove from skillet and keep warm.

Saute onion and mushrooms in the remaining butter.

Add the wine and boullion cube.

Add the Turkey slices and simmer for 15 min.

Remove the Turkey and pour sauce over it.

Sprinkle parsley on top.

Serve with rice, your favorite green vegetable and Pat Paulsen Chardonnay.

great at a State dinner !

Pat Paulsen

Child Abuse Prevention Society*
"Help us put the 'cap' on child abuse!"

CHICKEN ENCHILADA CASSEROLE

```
8   ½-chicken breasts
2   bell peppers
Large can of corn
½ lb of Jack cheese, sliced
1 dozen tortillas, corn
6   onions
6   large tomatoes
  2 cups milk
Oil, flour, hot sauce to taste
```

First, cut the tortillas in half and fry in oil til crisp. Put on paper towels to drain. Bake the chicken with 2 sliced onions; season with salt, pepper,and garlic salt. (Place the chicken on the onions and bake at 350 for 1 hour.) When the chicken is cooked, remove skin and bones and cut into slices and put aside.

Slice remaining onions and green peppers, and saute with tomatoes in oiled pan for about 15 minutes, then add 2 cupsof milk to sauce. When this is well mixed, add flour to thicken slightly.

Layer into a greased casserole - first the tortillas then the chicken strips and corn and then the sauce and then start over with the tortillas/ top with sliced cheese.

Cook for one half hour in a 350 oven

Makes a most delicious "put in the freezer and save for unexpected guests" dish.

Serve with a mixed green salad - and of course- a chocolate dessert!

Lois Pavlow - President

Child Abuse Prevention Society
Pier 23, Embarcadero, San Francisco, California 94111 • (415) 567-7027

*a non-profit organization

159 EAST BLITHEDALE
MILL VALLEY CALIFORNIA 94941
TELEPHONE (415) 381-5400

REALRESTAURANTS

Grilled Stuffed Pasilla or Poblano Peppers
With Avocado Salsa

The avocado salsa:

2 small avocados, diced and tossed in a little lemon juice
6 tablespoons olive oil
2 tablespoons Japanese rice-wine vinegar
1 tablespoon chopped cilantro
1 tablespoon chopped scallions
   Salt to taste
   Dash of Shaoxing rice wine or dry sherry

The peppers:

6 Pasilla or Poblano peppers
12 ounces of mixed Jarlsberg, Asiago, Jack or other meltable, non-
   stringy cheeses (goat cheese is excellent)
3 tablespoons minced scallions
   Salt and black pepper to taste.

1. To make the salsa, put the avocado in a small mixing bowl. Place
the remaining ingredients in a jar and shake to combine as you would a
vinaigrette. Mix with the avocado and set aside.
2. Cut the tops off the peppers and save them. Remove the seeds. Par
boil both the tops and bottoms for about one minute. They should remain
crisp. Run them under cold water, dry thoroughly and stuff semi-firmly
with the cheese. Fasten the tops back on with a toothpick and grill over
medium coals, turning them as necessary, for about four minutes or until
the cheese melts. (This is best done on an angled grill so the cheese
won't run out.) Serve one to a plate with the avocado salsa.

Yield: Six servings.

MUSTARDS GRILL
THE RIO GRILL
FOG CITY DINER

THE BEST COOKIE IN THE WORLD

(No kidding!)

I hate to part with this fantastic recipe, but anything for the San Francisco Ballet, so here it is:

"Döler"

1 cup	Sugar
1 cup	Butter
1 cup	Cream, whipped
1 cup	Potato flour
1 1/2 cup	Almonds, blanched and chopped
1 tsp.	Vanilla sugar (Scandinavian food stores)

Stir butter and sugar until white, add whipped cream,
then flour, vanilla sugar and chopped almonds. Spoon
dough (experiment with a few first) with teaspoon
on greased tin; bake until pale golden, 350°F.

Good luck!

POCKET OPERA

The Agricultural Bldg.
101 Embarcadero South,
Suite 101
San Francisco, CA 94105
(415) 398-2220

Donald Pippin
Music Director

Dino DiDonato
General Manager

PIPPIN'S QUICK PASTA SAUCE

Serves from 2 baritones to 6 sopranos

Ingredients:

2 tbls.	Butter
¼ cup	Olive oil
3 cloves	Garlic, chopped fine
1 small	Yellow onion, chopped
1 cup	Sliced fresh mushrooms
1 small	Japanese eggplant- cut into ½" slices
1 can or	Italian Style tomato paste
6-8	Roma tomatoes-skinned & seeded
1½ cups	Chicken stock
1 cup	White wine

Salt
Pepper

Directions:

1. In a large saucepan, heat together, the oil and butter. Meanwhile, bring the chicken stock to a boil.

2. Add the garlic, onion, mushrooms and eggplant to the butter/oil and sauté until the garlic turns golden. Add the tomato paste/tomatoes immediately.

3. Slowly stir in the hot chicken broth, more for a thin sauce, less for a thick one. Add the white wine.

4. Let simmer uncovered, on a low flame, for 20-30 minutes, stirring occasionally.

5. Add salt and pepper to taste before pouring over a pound of fettucini or spaghetti.

   "This recipe is best for late night and after performance meals--especially for opera and performing arts groups on tight catering budgets. Be sure to have plenty of parmeseano and romano cheese on hand, and a loaf or two of hot sourdough bread. To complete the meal, you need a good, robust, old fashioned, North Beach, inexpensive Chianti. Buon Apetito!"

Donald Pippin

Examiner

This culinary oddity is heaven-sent for busy people who don't have time to do a whole lot of fussing, but still want something nice for dessert. It's made in one container and baked in another, so clean up chores are minimal. As it bakes, the ingredients separate all by themselves into a crust, a filling, and a browned top.

IMPOSSIBLE PIE

5 eggs

1/2 cup sugar

2 cups milk

1/2 cup flour

1 cup shredded coconut

2 tablespoons melted butter

2 teaspoons flavoring (almond, vanilla, or lemon are nice)

whipped cream or crushed berries for topping (optional)

In a blender, mix all the ingredients except the whipped cream or fruit in the order listed. Pour into a lightly greased, 9-inch pie pan. Bake in a preheated, 350-degree oven for about 40 to 45 minutes, or until a knife inserted in the center comes out clean. Top with whipped cream and/or berries. Serves 6 to 8.

Enjoy,

Bea Pixa

The San Francisco Examiner • 110 Fifth Street • P.O. Box 7260 • San Francisco, CA 94120 • (415) 777-2424

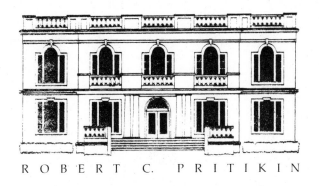

R O B E R T C. P R I T I K I N

HAM AND EGGS TO DIE FOR.

This effortless concoction will make you the king or queen of the brunch bunch. The beauty of this baked, steaming egg fantasy is that you can prepare it in advance of your brunch or lunch, put it on the buffet and forget it while the guests gorge themselves for an hour or more. Be prepared -- they come back for thirds.

Ingredients for 8 guests.

24 hard-cooked eggs; 3 ten oz. cans White Sauce; 2 cups grated cheddar cheese; 2 cups ham cubes the size of tiny dice; 4 tablespoons margarine; 1/2 cup sliced black olives; 4 dashes tabasco sauce; 2 tablespoons Worcestershire sauce; 2 tablespoons curry powder.

Get a wire egg slicer and slice your hard-cooked eggs. Then dump them into a casserole dish along with the tiny ham cubes and sliced olives. Now, melt the margarine in a large sauce pan and throw in the three cans of white sauce. Naturally, the flame is on. Stir out the lumps and when the sauce is smooth and bubbling contentedly add the tabasco, Worcestershire and curry. Now, throw in all but 1/2 cup of the cheddar cheese and stir until the cheese melts into the mixture. Then transfer the sauce to the baking dish and blend the whole mess together. Sprinkle remaining grated cheese on top. Bake at 375 for one half hour.

YOUR GUESTS ARE CERTAIN TO EXCLAIM WITH ALL
THE "Y" WORDS: YIPPIE! YUMMY! YOWIE!

Robert C Pritikin

47 CHENERY STREET   SAN FRANCISCO CA 94131   PHONE: (415) 824-4458

ZINATALIA LAMB

1/2 cup oil (preferably olive)
1/8 cup sesame oil
1/4 cup red wine vinegar
1/2 cup Zinfandel wine (preferably cheap)
1/8 cup light soy sauce
4 oz. chopped green chiles (preferably hot)
6 cloves of garlic, mashed
2 tsps. oregano
1 tsp. tarragon
1 tsp. basil
2 tbls. hot mustard
5-6 pounds of lamb steaks, or boned
    and butterflied leg of lamb
1-8oz. can tomato sauce
3 tbls. honey

Mix the first twelve ingredients and marinate lamb
overnight in covered dish, turning once. Remove
meat and add tomato sauce and honey to marinade
sauce, mixing very well. Use to baste meat.

Barbeque over hot, hot double layer of coals,
basting regularly until done to your liking.
DON'T OVERCOOK!

G. Kirk Raab
President and Chief Operating Officer

Louise H. Renne,
City Attorney

PECAN PIE

3/4 cup brown sugar

1 cup white Karo syrup

1 cup pecan meats, cut small

2 tablespoons cornstarch

2 eggs

1 teaspoon vanilla

1 teaspoon butter

Beat eggs, add sugar, cornstarch, Karo syrup; then nuts, vanilla and butter.

Beat 2 minutes and pour into unbaked pie shell.

Bake 10 minutes at 450°, then 50 minutes at 325°.

Mrs. E.E. Bickham
A Roundup of Recipes

Sincerely,

Louise H. Renne
City Attorney

LHR:kz

CROWN RACK OF LAMB & COMPOTE

INGREDIENTS:

CROWN RACK OF LAMB
4 Rack of Lamb
6 Cups of Virgin Olive Oil
4 White Onions
4 Bay leaves
10-15 Whole PepperCorns
2-3 Branches of Rosemary
½ Clove of Garlic
3-4 Branches of Fresh Mint
Honey (English Heather)

COMPOTE
Fifth of Brandy
16 Apricots
8 Pears
6 Cinnamon Sticks
½ Cup of Cloves
Juice of 1 Lemon
Juice of 1 Orange
1 Cup of Sugar

PREPARATION:

1. Prepare marinade with finely-ground Onions; crush Garlic; add herbs and toss into shallow pan with Olive Oil. Marinate Lamb Racks overnight.

2. Remove Lamb Racks from marinade, place side-by-side and sew together; pull into crown and wrap with string. Place crown in shallow roasting pan, season with salt and pepper, then rub with Honey glaze.

3. Roast in pre-heated oven (375°) for 30 to 35 minutes -- depending on taste (rare to medium rare). Re-glaze every 10 minutes. Before serving, decorate with paper caps.

4. Prepare Compote by peeling Apricots and Pears (leave stems on Pears).

5. Place fruit in baking dish filled with a syrup of Brandy, Sugar, Spices, Lemon and Orange Juices. Poach in oven until medium-cooked.

6. When ready to serve, place Apricots in center of crown and sprinkle Rosemary leaves on top. Decorate serving platter with poached Pears and Rosemary leaves.

Serve with chilled Monterey Vineyard Chardonnay.

My favorite for that very "special" Dinner

Dick Revnes

One Maritime Plaza San Francisco, CA 94111 Telephone 415 956 7200 Telex 278532

162

SPAGHETTI WITH MUSSELS, SCALLOPS AND SHRIMP

In a skillet over medium heat, cook <u>1 large onion</u>, chopped in <u>3 Tbs. olive oil</u> until light golden. Add <u>2 cloves garlic</u>, minced, and cook another 30 seconds. Stir in <u>1/2 cup dry white wine</u>, <u>1 1/2 Tbs. fresh basil</u>, minced, or <u>1 1/2 tsp. dried</u>, <u>1 Tbs. fresh marjoram</u>, minced, or 1 tsp dried, and cook 1 minute. Add <u>1 1/2 cups fresh tomatoes</u>, peeled, seeded and chopped, or canned Italian plum tomatoes, drained. Increase the heat and simmer 5 minutes.

In another pan bring 4-5 quarts salted water to a boil Add <u>1 lb. spaghetti</u>, and cook until it is just tender. Drain. While the spaghetti is cooking, bring the tomato mixture to a boil and add <u>1 1/2 lb. mussels</u>, scrubbed and debearded, (or 2 lb. clams, scrubbed), cover and cook until the shells open, approximately 5 minutes. Add <u>1 lb. sea scallops</u>, halved and <u>1 lb. large shrimp</u>, peeled, and deveined. Cover and cook an additional 2-3 minutes until scallops and shrimp are barely firm. Season to taste with <u>salt and pepper</u>.

Place the drained spaghetti on a warm serving plate, toss with some of the seafood sauce, and pour over the rest of the seafood with its sauce. Serves 6-8. MSR

Mary SRisky

BRUNO RISTOW, M.D.

2100 Webster Street, Suite 502
Pacific Presbyterian Professional Building
San Francisco, California 94115
Telephone 415-923-3003

Chief, Plastic & Reconstructive Surgery
Pacific Presbyterian Medical Center

Fellow American College of Surgeons
Certified American Board of Plastic Surgery

FAROFA

4	Tablespoons butter or margarine
2	Tablespoons onion thinly sliced
1	Cup Manioc meal

Melt butter in skillet and saute onion. When onion is translucent and butter is bubbling add manioc meal and keep stirring at medium heat. The farofa is almost ready when it has the consistency of toasted bread crumbs. To finish, add either one of the following: fresh chopped parsely, chopped prunes or raisins, chopped olives or chopped hardboiled eggs.

Farofa is the most classic of Brazilian side dishes. It is always served with Feijoada, the national dish. Frequently it accompanies steak or chicken. It is equally delicious with pork roast, especially with the prune or raisin variety. Farofa like truffles adds a special taste to almost any food.

Brazil is larger than the continental United States, as such it is easy to understand why its many regional cuisines are entirely different from one another. African, Indian and Portuguese influences run strongly. Farofa, however from the deep jungle of the Amazon to the Southern plains of the gauchos, from the wealthiest to the simplest table, is the unifying side dish.

BRUNO RISTOW, M.D.

URANIA RISTOW

THE DONATELLO

RAVIOLI AI FRUTTI DI MARE DEL BUONGUSTAIO

HOMEMADE RAVIOLI FILLED WITH PRAWNS, LOBSTER, AND SCALLOPS IN A LOBSTER SAUCE

Filling Ingredients

1	Maine lobster (live) 1 to 1-1/4 lbs.	
1/4	lb. scallops	1/4 lb. prawns, cleaned
1/2	bunch chives, finely chopped	1 clove garlic, finely chopped
1/4	cup bread crumbs	1 shallot, finely chopped
1/2	lemon	1/4 cup lobster sauce
		Salt and pepper to taste

Dismember lobster by first twisting tail off. Then remove claws and body from shell. Remove meat from tail. Remove claws and body from shell and reserve for sauce. Grind all seafood coarsely, and saute in butter. Mix in garlic, chives and shallot and saute two minutes. Add remaining ingredients and chill.

Lobster Sauce Ingredients

Body and claws of lobster
3 Tbl. tomato sauce
1 carrot
Pinch of tarragon and thyme

2 cups white wine
1/2 small onion
2 Tbl. brandy
Salt and pepper to taste

Grind lobster, onions and carrots. Saute for 3-4 minutes, then add remaining ingredients. Cook for 15-20 minutes or until reduced by half. Correct seasonings and strain.

Pasta Recipe

3 eggs
2 1/2 cups all purpose flour
Pinch of salt

Form a well in the middle of the flour. Add eggs and salt and with a fork, combine until it can be worked by hand. Knead until flour is incorporated and pasta forms a smooth, elastic ball. If too wet, add more flour.

Assembly

Roll the pasta out flat to 1/8" thickness. Cut into 2" squares with a fluted pasta cutter. Place a heaping teaspoon of filling in one corner of the square. Brush the pasta with water or egg yolk and fold in a triangular fashion and seal. Refrigerate for 1/2 hour.

To Cook Ravioli

Reduce the remaining lobster sauce with an equal amount of heavy cream until thick. Bring 3 quarts of salted water to a boil. Add ravioli and cook 2-3 minutes or until they rise to the surface. Drain and add to sauce with chopped parsley and serve immediately. (Serves 4)

Five Hundred & One Post Street • San Francisco, California 94102 • (415) 441-7100 • Telex 172875

ALBERT L. ROSEN
PRESIDENT AND GENERAL MANAGER

GRAND MARNIER ICE CREAM SOUFFLE

Soften 1/2 gallon vanilla ice cream
Mix with 48 crumbled macaroons
8 tbsp. Grand Marnier
2 cups whipped cream
Pour into large springform pan
Top with 1 tbsp. powdered sugar
   and 1/2 cup chopped pecans
Freeze the mixture

Topping:
Heat together:
1 pkg. frozen strawberries
1 pkg. frozen raspberries
4 tbsp. Grand Marnier
Pour over each serving.

Not for those who want to watch their calories, but
as for a taste treat, this dessert is incomparable.

San Francisco Progress Serving San Francisco, South San Francisco, Daly City, San Bruno

"My favorite recipe"

Many years ago, when I brought a visiting columnist from the Pittsburgh Press home for dinner, on short notice, my wife concocted this sauce to jazz up the chicken legs and thighs. Since then, the "accident" is a favorite.

Jack Rosenbaum

Basting sauce for chicken legs and thighs:

Ingredients:
10 chicken legs & thighs (left whole)
½ cup soy sauce
1 tsp salad oil
3 or 4 cloves garlic, pressed
1 tbsp white wine
1 tsp (rounded) Herbes de Provence.

Preparation:
Remove as much fat from chicken as possible (do not skin), rinse and pat dry with paper towels. Place skin side down on broiler rack which has been covered with foil.

Sauce:
Mix soy sauce, oil, pressed garlic, wine & herbs. Brush chicken with sauce. Broil approximately 30 minutes, then turn and brush other side with sauce. Broil another 15 or 20 minutes or until chicken tests done.

Jack Rosenbaum

MAIN OFFICE:
851 Howard Street
San Francisco, CA 94103
415/982-8022
Classified: 415/495-8000

SAN BRUNO OFFICE:
715 El Camino Real
San Bruno, CA 94066
Advertising: 415/583-0876
Editorial: 415/588-3392

SALADE ALGERIENNE

5 ripe tomatoes
8 green bell peppers
5 large garlic cloves
1 tablespoon tomato paste
1 touch paprika
1 touch nutmeg
1 sugar cube
2 oz. vegetable oil
salt, black pepper

Pre-heat oven to 400°, place tomatoes and bell peppers on a cookie sheet. Remove tomatoes after skin starts to peel (2-3 minutes), remove bell peppers after skin starts to peel (5 minutes). Skin tomatoes and bell peppers. <u>Dice</u> tomatoes and drain in a collander. <u>Slice</u> bell peppers ½" wide. Drain and remove.

Put tomatoes in a pan and heat slowly, until liquid evaporates. Add sugar cube, tomato paste, bell peppers, salt and pepper to taste, and a touch of nutmeg and paprika. Cover the pan for 15 minutes. Stir occasionally with a wooden spoon. Add the oil and the chopped garlic and let cook over very low heat for about one half hour.

You could add a little cayenne if you like it spicy. You can serve it cold or hot.

Claude Rouas

Claude Rouas

180 Rutherford Hill Road Rutherford, California 94573 Telephone (707) 963•1211

OLYMPIA OYSTER LOAF

About 25 Olympia oysters per person.

Drain oysters. Marinate them in beaten eggs, lemon juice.

Drain. Combine very fine breadcrumbs and flour ($\frac{1}{2}$ & $\frac{1}{2}$),
salt and pepper. Roll oysters carefully in breadcrumb
mixture. Lay out oysters on a platter. Fry them in a pan,
in plenty of butter -- about $\frac{1}{2}$ minute. Lay them on absorbent
paper.

French bread rolls: One per person. Cut off top and scoop
out middle. Butter inside well. Put on tops and put rolls
in oven. Heat well. Put oysters into cut rolls.

Serve with wedges of lemon and hot catsup.

Madeleine H Russell

Tomm Ruud

RIGO JANCSI, *or a fix for a Chocoholic*
Chocolate Cream Slices

(to make 35 cream slices)

This is the perfect Chocolate recipe, because it contains more Chocolate than any other ingredient.

The Cake

2 T butter
2 T flour
3 oz. unsweetened chocolate
3/4 C. (1½ quarter-pound sticks)
  unsalted butter, softened

½ C. sugar
4 eggs, separated
Pinch of salt
½ C. sifted all-purpose flour

Preheat the oven to 350°. With a pastry brush or paper towel, butter an 11-by-17-inch jelly-roll pan and sprinkle the flour over the butter. Tap the edge of the pan on a table to knock out the excess flour.

Melt the chocolate over low heat in a heavy 1-quart saucepan or in the top of a double boiler placed over simmering water. Set the chocolate aside to cool to lukewarm. Cream the butter and ¼ C. of the sugar by beating them against the side of a mixing bowl with a wooden spoon, continuing to beat until the mixture is light and fluffy. Add the melted chocolate and beat in the egg yolks, one at a time.

In another mixing bowl preferably of unlined copper, beat the egg whites and a pinch of salt with a wire whisk or rotary beater until the whites cling to the beater; add the remaining ¼ C. of sugar and beat until the whites form stiff, unwavering peaks. With a rubber spatula, stir about 1/3 of the whites into the chocolate base, then pour the chocolate mixture over the rest of the whites. Sprinkle the flour lightly on top. Gently fold the flour into the mixture until no white streaks are visible.

Pour the batter into the prepared jelly-roll pan, spreading it evenly with a rubber spatula. Bake in the middle of the oven for 15 to 18 minutes, or until the cake shrinks slightly away from the sides of the pan and a knife inserted in the middle comes out clean. Remove the cake from the oven, loosen it from the pan by running a sharp knife around the sides, and turn it out on a rack to cool.

The Filling

1½ C. heavy cream
10 oz. semisweet chocolate,
  broken or chopped into small
  chunks

4 T. dark rum
1 t. vanilla extract

I usually double the filling.

In a heavy 1-quart saucepan, combine the cream and chocolate, and stir over medium heat until the chocolate dissolves. Then reduce the heat to very low and simmer, stirring almost constantly, until the mixture thickens into a heavy cream. Pour it into a bowl and refrigerate for at least 1 hour. When the mixture is very cold, pour in the rum and vanilla and beat with a wire whisk or a rotary or electric beater until the filling is smooth and creamy and forms soft peaks when the beater is lifted from the bowl. Do not overbeat or the cream will turn into butter.

Cut the cake in half to make two layers, each 8½ inches wide. Over one layer spread the filling, which will be about 2 inches thick. Set the other layer on top. Refrigerate on a rack for about 1 hour.

The Glaze

1 C. fine granulted sugar
1/3 C. water

7 oz. semisweet chocolate, broken or
  chopped into small chunks

While the cake is refrigerating, make the glaze. In a heavy 1-quart saucepan, heat the sugar, water and chocolate over medium heat, stirring constantly, until the sugar and chocolate are dissolved. Remove the pan from the heat, cover and let the glaze cool for about 20 minutes.

Set the rack holding the cake on a jelly-roll pan and, holding the saucepan with the glaze 2 inches above the cake, pour the glaze over it. Refrigerate the cake on the rack 20 minutes longer, or tomil the glaze is firm.

Serve by cutting it into 35 small equal pieces, 5 in each row across and 7 in each row down. Use a sharp knife that has been dipped in warm water. Rinse the knife and dip it again in warm water before each cutting.

enjoy!
Tomm Ruud

170

It happens that beets and yams are two of my favorite foods, so
I combined them with another favorite food, ginger, thus creating
Salad à la Salkind. It's a little different, and colorful.

Salad à la Salkind

1 lb. beets
3 small yams
½ Tbsp slivered orange zest
4 Tbsp orange juice
3 Tbsp raspberry vinegar
1 Tbsp Hazelnut oil
½ Tbsp olive oil
1½ tsp slivered lemon zest
1½ tsp minced ginger

Wash beets. Cut off all but 1 inch of tops. Wrap each beet in foil
and bake in 400 oven until done -- generally takes 1 to 1½ hours. As
soon as cool enough to handle, peel and slice into 1/8 inch rounds.
While beets are cooling, thoroughly combine orange zest, orange juice,
vinegar, Hazelnut oil and olive oil. As soon as beets are peeled,
pour marinade mixture over them and cool. Refrigerate overnight.
Steam the yams until they are just done -- approximately 40 minutes.
Cool, peel and slice into 1/8 inch rounds.

On individual salad plates, put 1½ Tbsp of the beet marinade mixture.
Arrange alternating slices of beets and yams. Place generous portion
of lemon zest on the beets and generous portion of ginger on the yams.

Serve. Makes 6 portions.

Milton Salkind

USVP

SCHLEIN MARKETING FUND

Philip S. Schlein
General Partner

HORS D'OEUVRE

SOPHIE'S ROMANIAN EGGPLANT

    1 Large Eggplant
    1/2 Medium Onion --- Coarsely Chopped
    2 Tablespoons Olive Oil
    Salt to Taste
    Pepper to Taste

                        Preheat Over 375°

  ° Pierce eggplant --- two/three times.
    Bake whole until very soft --- approximately 1 1/2 hours.

  ° Scoop out and mash while warm, pulp and juice.

  ° Add to pulp onion, olive oil, and salt and pepper to taste.

  ° Marinate several hours.

  ° Serve on bite-size pieces of Rye Bread.

As a child in my grandmother's kitchen I learned this recipe —— while tearfully chopping the onions.

Phil Schlein

2180 Sand Hill Road Suite 300 Menlo Park, Calif. 94025 (415) 854-9080

Adolph Schuman
FOR
Lilli Ann

Here's a dish I sometimes prepare when friends are coming over.
It will serve four as a side dish or two hungry people as a
main course with a tossed green salad and French bread accompaniment.

JO'S CLAM FETTUCCINI

Ingredients:

1 pint	sour cream
6 ozs.	fresh cream
3/4 cup	chopped green onions
1 cup	sliced small fresh mushrooms
2 - 6 oz. cans	chopped clams with juice reserved
1/2 tsp.	white pepper
1 Tbsp.	Good Seasons Classic Herbs salad dressing mix
3/4 of 10 oz.	package Golden Grain fettuccini
1/2 cup	fresh grated Parmesan cheese
1 Tbsp.	olive oil
	salt and nutmeg, to taste

In large 10" saute pan, stir over low heat until warm the sour cream
and fresh cream. Add the green onions, mushrooms, clams and juice,
white pepper and dressing mix. Let simmer for 1/2 hour, stirring
occasionally.

In a large pot, boil water for the pasta, adding the olive oil and
salt to taste. Bring to a rolling boil. Add fettuccini, stirring
to prevent sticking. Cook until tender, about 10 minutes.

Drain fettuccini and pour it into the pan with sauce. Let simmer
on low for 10 minutes, stirring occasionally.

Place in warmed serving dish, sprinkle top with Parmesan cheese, and
enjoy!

Jo Schuman

Creme de Tomate Marie-Louise
[Cream of Tomato Soup]

1 Tbsp. butter
1 Tbsp. flour   3½ c
1 can (1¾ pt.) tomato juice
pepper, salt, cinnamon, lemon peel
   twist, stalk of celery with tops,
   parsley root or chopped parsley

1 tsp. sugar
pinch baking soda
½ cup milk

Melt one healthy tablespoon of butter and add one tablespoon flour. Stir well over medium flame. DO NOT let butter brown. Add can of tomato juice.

Season to taste with pepper, salt, cinnamon, lemon peel twist, stalk of celery with tops, parsley root or chopped parsley.

Add one teaspoon of sugar and stir.

Bring to a boil, then simmer until well flavored. Skim to remove vegetables and lemon peel.

Place in double boiler until ready to serve. When ready to serve, add a pinch of baking soda and 1/2 cup milk. Stir gently over low flame.   Serves 3.

James Schwabacher

SAM'S GRILL, INC.
374 BUSH ST.   421-0594
SAN FRANCISCO, CA 94104

CONEY ISLAND CLAM CHOWDER

24 fresh medium size clams or
1/2 lb. pkg. frozen clams
4 cups water
1 large onion, minced
1/2 stalk celery, cleaned, diced
1 green pepper, cleaned, diced
1/4 cup cooking oil
2 tbsp. flour
2 medium sized potatoes, peeled and diced
1 1/2 cups stewed tomatoes
salt to taste

Boil clams in water till they open, drain, reserving liquid and
shuck them. Set aside.
In soup kettle heat oil, add minced onion, celery and pepper,
braise until transparent looking (tender) stirring constantly,
dust with flour, stir. Add boiling clam broth, (make sure broth
is hot before adding to kettle) stir til smooth and bring to soft
boil. Dice stewed tomatoes and add with liquid to soup. Bring
to boil again and add diced potatoes; continue to simmer til
potatoes are tender, 10-15 minutes. Add clams, salt to taste and
bring to last boil. Serve with salt crackers.

SKI CABIN LENTIL SOUP

This is the sort of thing a restaurant critic likes to eat on a night off--something hearty, easy to make, and as far removed from California cuisine as possible.

    1½ pounds very spicy Italian or Louisiana sausage
    1 pound of dried lentils
    1 large chopped onion
    As many garlic cloves as you can stand peeling
    4 stalks celery, chopped
    8 Italian plum tomatoes and juices
    2 bay leaves
    1 small can tomato paste
    1/3 cup extra virgin olive oil
    1 teaspoon cayenne
    1 teaspoon ground black pepper
    2 tablespoons red wine vinegar

Wash the lentils and place in a soup pot with warm water to cover. Let stand for a couple of hours, then bring to a boil. Add the onions, garlic, celery, tomatoes and tomato paste. Cover and simmer for one hour. Slice and toss in the sausage.

Add the bay leaf, cayenne, black pepper and olive oil and continue to simmer, covered, for an hour or two, until very thick. Add vinegar toward the end.

Stan Sesser

(415) 777-1111

This cake is a delicious, quick alternative to fruit tarts, pies and even better than the pineapple upside-down cake of memory. You can substitute almost any tart fruit for the oranges; however if you decide to use fresh pineapple, cook it first.

Blood Orange Upside-down Cake

4 T. butter (2 oz.)
3/4 c. light brown sugar
1/2 c. soft butter (4 oz.)
1 c. sugar
2 egg yolks
1 t. vanilla
1 1/2 c. flour
2 t. baking powder (home-made or non-aluminum type such as Rumfords)
1/4 t. salt (omit if using salted butter)
2 egg whites
1/4 t. cream of tartar

1/2 c. milk
approximately 2 lbs. blood oranges

Pre-heat oven to 350°. Slice skins and white pith from oranges, keeping them as round as possible. Melt the 4 T. butter with the brown sugar in a 9" round cake pan or black iron skillet. Slice the oranges about 3/8" thick crosswise and arrange the slices in the prepared pan, overlapping them as necessary. For the cake, cream the 1/2 c. butter with the sugar until light. Beat in the yolks and vanilla until light again. Mix the dry ingredients together and add them alternately with the milk; beat just until smooth. Beat the room temperature egg whites until they are foamy, add the cream of tartar and beat until they hold soft peaks. Fold about one quarter of the whites into the batter to lighten it and fold in the rest. Spread over the fruit in the pan. At this point the cake can wait an hour or two unless you've used home-made baking powder. Bake 30 to 40 minutes or until the cake is golden brown and firm. Cool 5 minutes and turn out onto a cake plate. Serve warm with slightly sweetened whipped cream.

Lindsey R. Shere

177

FROM THE KITCHEN OF

PHYLLIS SILVERSTEIN

Ginger Roll

4 eggs
1 c. Sugar
2 Tabl. orange juice
1 Tabl. grated orange rind
1 c. Flour

1 teas Baking powder
1 teas. ground ginger
1/2 teas cinnamon
1/2 teas salt.

Beat eggs for 10 min, until thick and creamy, gradually beat in 1 c. sugar and continue beating until mixture is smooth. Stir in orange juice + grated orange rind. Combine flour with baking powder, ginger and cinnamon and salt. Sift the flour mixture over the top of the egg mixture + Fold the flour in gently but thoroughly. Pour batter into a 10" x 15" jelly roll pan, lined with oiled wax paper + bake in 375° oven for 15 to 17 mins. — or until it begins to pull away from the sides of the pan

Turn cake out on a dish towel. Gently strip off the wax paper — roll up the cake lengthwise using the dish towel to roll it. Cool. Unroll the cake + spread the surface thickly with:

1 c. heavy cream whipped
3/4 c. ginger marmalade } combine

Reroll the cake + glaze the surface with 1/3 c. ginger marmalade, heated until it is of spreading consistency.

Decorate with mint leaves.

This cake was served at the opening S.F. Ballet Auxiliary meeting — I received many requests for the receipt — Hope you enjoy it —

Phyllis

Steven M. Somers
Chairman, C.E.O.

This has always been one of our favorite dessert recipes because it looks pretty, is easy to make and, best of all, ends the evening with a "giggle" (considering the amount of Kahlua that is used).

Two years ago, it became even more special since it captured first prize at the March of Dimes Gourmet Gala.

Fresh Fruit with Kahlua Sauce

Ingredients:

Fresh fruit
  (i.e.) Sliced apple, pineapple, grapes, bananas, strawberries, etc.

1	8 oz.	cream cheese softened
1	Cup	non-dairy whipped cream
3/4	Cup	brown sugar
1/3	Cup	Kahlua
1	Cup	Sour Cream

Mix cream cheese and whipped cream. Set aside. Mix brown sugar and Kahlua over low heat until well blended. Add cream cheese mixture. Mix well. Add sour cream. Beat until creamy.

Arrange sliced fruit on large platter, using Kahlua sauce for dipping.

The sauce should be made in advance and refrigerated two days before serving.

Examiner

CHOCOLATE MOUSSE

This is a dessert that demands you forget all diets and will power. Just eat, enjoy, and ignore all the guilt.

Crust: 1 pkg. Nabisco chocolate wafers; 1 cube butter melted

Filling: 1 12-oz. pkg. Nestle chocolate chips, 6 eggs, 3 c. whipping cream

1. Crush wafers, mix in melted butter, line bottom and sides of 9-inch springform pan with mixture, bake 10 minutes in 350 degree oven, remove and let cool.

2. Melt chocolate chips in top of double boiler, stirring occasionally.

3. When chocolate chips have metled, add 2 eggs, one at a time, and 4 egg yolks, one at a time, while double boiler still over the heat, beating hard after each addition.

4. Remove from top of double boiler and allow to cool.

5. Beat 4 egg whites until they are stiff.

6. Whip 2 cups whipping cream until peaks form.

7. Fold egg whites into chocolate mixture gently, but thoroughly, and when smooth and creamy, fold into whipping cream. Pour mixture onto crust and refrigerate at least 2 hours.

8. For decoration, whip remaining cup of whipping cream, put into pastry bag and work onto mousse. Make chocolate leaves by melting bittersweet chocolate, covering back side of a camellia leaf, placing in freezer for one hour, removing and peeling off gently. Place leaf on top.

Art Spander
sports columnist

The San Francisco Examiner ● 110 Fifth Street ● San Francisco, CA. 94103 ● (415) 777-2424

David Standridge
Senior Executive Vice President

FAMOUS BEANS

These spicy beans are great as a side dish or a main course.
They're terrific for back yard get-togethers and tailgate
parties. A wonderful do ahead dish as they taste even better
the next day.

2	pounds pinto beans
2	bunches green onions, chopped
1	large white onion, chopped
4	cloves garlic, chopped
3	tablespoons bacon drippings
2	pounds ground pork sausage
½	cup chili powder
1	tablespoon salt
1	10-ounce can mixed tomatoes and green chilies*
1	10-ounce can salsa (mild)
1	pound pepperoni, thinly sliced

Wash pinto beans and soak overnight (at least 12 hours) in
enough water to cover.

Saute onions and garlic in bacon drippings in a large pan
over medium heat until onions are soft. Add pork sausage,
breaking it up into small pieces. Add remaining ingredients.
Cook for 20-30 minutes, covered.

*The best brand is Ro-tel Tomatoes and Green Chilies, but
you can substitute 1 10-ounce can stewed tomatoes mixed
with 1 4-ounce can diced green chilies. If you do substitute,
increase chili powder by ¼ cup and add 1 seeded, diced
jalapeno pepper.

Serves 12, soak overnight, preparation time 30 minutes,
cook 2 hours.

Old Fashioned Pot Roast

3½ to 4 pound eye of the round
4 carrots, sliced
2 turnips, cut in half
2 onions, sliced
½ pound mushrooms
½ teaspoon oregano, crushed
1½ tablespoons green peppercorns
1 strip each of lemon and orange peel
1¼ cups of Pinot Noir
3/4 cup of beef stock or broth
salt and pepper to taste
2 tablespoons oil

Rub the meat with the salt, pepper, and oregano. Heat
the oil in a heavy casserole or dutch oven. Brown the
meat on all sides. Add the vegetables, the orange and
lemon peel, the wine and broth. Bake in a 350 oven for
4 hours (cover the pot).

Remove the meat and vegetables. Place the pan over
medium heat and thicken sauce with a little cornstarch mixed
in water. Add the green peppercorns. Slice the meat
across the grain and arrange on a platter with the
vegetables and pour some of the sauce over the meat.
Serve the remaining sauce in a gravy boat.

(415) 777-1111

MELVIN M. SWIG
Fairmont Hotel
SAN FRANCISCO 94106

DATE PUDDING

1/2 cup nuts
1/2 cup milk
1 cup flour
1 tsp baking powder
1 cup sugar
1/2 cup chopped dates
1 tsp vanilla

Sift flour and baking powder together; add sugar, milk, dates and nuts. Batter will be stiff.

Bring to a boil 1-1/2 cups brown sugar, 1-1/2 cups water, 2 tsps butter, 1 tsp vanilla. Pour into baking dish. Drop the batter one tsp at a time into syrup mixture. Bake 30 or 40 minutes in 375 oven.

Cool and top with cream, whipped or otherwise.

CHESTNUT SOUP

1 lb chestnuts
6 cups chicken stock

Cut a cross on chestnuts and par boil for 5 minutes, peel and add the chicken broth.

Brown lightly in 2 tbsp of oil 10 minutes or until soft: 3 medium carrots, 2 medium onions, 1 celery rib (chopped). Add to chestnut and chicken broth. Cook until chestnuts are soft, about 30 minutes. Puree in Cuisinart. Return to kettle. Add 1 cup heavy cream, salt, white pepper, 1/4 tsp mace and bring to boil.

May be eaten hot or cold.

SPANISH RICE

Boil 1 lb. rice and strain - DO NOT BLANCHE

Stew together for 1 hour:

    1 cup olive oil
    2 green peppers
    5 large onions
    ½ stalk celery
    1 large can tomatoes (solid packed)
    4 oz. can mushrooms - slices or stems and pieces, strained
    1 can tomato paste
    2 small chili peppers (finely minced)
    Salt to taste
    2 cloves garlic - grated fine or pressed

Bake 1 hour at 325°.

45 Belden San Francisco California 94104 415 956-3222

RICHARD TAM

my favorite sunday lunch

<u>TOMATO BEEF CHOW MEIN</u>
serves 4

1 lb all-egg thin sliced fresh noodles
1 lb flank steak sliced diagonally

soy sauce	2 med tomatoes wedged
balsamic vinegar	1 onion wedged
brown sugar	1 green pepper wedged then blanched
sesame oil	2 stalks of celery, cut diagonally
corn oil	1 clove of garlic, crushed
saké	1 lg can of tomato sauce
cornstarch	salt, pepper

1   Boil noodles in a large pot of salted water, ½lb at a
    time (1-2 minutes); when noodles surface, they are
    done. Spread onto cookie sheet rubbed with 2 tblsp of
    corn oil and 1 teasp of sesame oil. Broil noodles
    until brown (watch carefully as they brown suddenly);
    then turn and brown other side (procedure 15 min max).
    Let cool, cut into sections and hold in warm (250°) oven.

2   Combine raw sliced flank steak, 1 tblsp balsamic
    vinegar, 2 tblsp brown sugar, a generous dash of soy
    and a smaller dash of sesame oil and of saké; salt and
    pepper and finally add 1 tblsp of cornstarch. Mix and
    let stand.

3   Heat 2 tblsp of corn oil in a heavy pan. Sauté onion
    and garlic, then add green pepper and celery. After
    a moment, add tomato wedges and 1 lg can of tomato
    sauce together with a generous dash of balsamic vinegar,
    a sprinkling of brown sugar, salt and pepper.

4   In a separate pan, heat 2 tblsp corn oil until very
    hot; sauté meat mixture quickly, and while still very
    rare, combine with the tomato-vegetable sauce.

5   Cover crisp noodles from oven with tomato beef and
    serve immediately.

*a family recipie passed to me from
my mother.*

Richard Tam

This recipe is great for the active man or woman who doesn't have alot of time to spend in the kitchen. However, your guests will swear that you have worked your fingers to the bone.

Chicken Liver Sauté

2 lbs.	fresh chicken livers
1 large	onion, diced
1/2 lb.	fresh mushrooms, sliced
1 cup	white wine
1 large	clove of garlic, chopped fine
1	package frozen peas
1/2 tsp.	pepper
1/4 tsp.	salt
1 cup	flour
4 Tbsp.	olive oil
dashes	paprika

In plastic bag place flour, salt and pepper, shaking to mix. Add the chicken livers and shake well until coated. Saute the onions and garlic in a large frying pan with the olive oil until slightly done and translucent. Add the floured livers and stir fry until nicely brown, 2-3 minutes. Add the sliced mushrooms and stir fry for another 2 minutes. Add the frozen peas and wine and simmer until the peas are cooked through. Season to taste with paprika.

If the gravy becomes too thick, dilute with a mixture of half wine and half water to obtain the proper consistency.

Great served over rice or noodles.

Jeanne Taylor

Lilli Ann Corporation • 2701 16th Street, San Francisco, California 94103 • (415) 863-2720

GLADYS S. THACHER
3979 WASHINGTON STREET
SAN FRANCISCO, CALIFORNIA
94118

This recipe, a family tradition, represents a collaborative effort that only improves with age and an extra dowsing of brandy. It came to me by way of two friends, and having passed it on to others, it is offered here as the _best_ persimmon pudding to toast many a festive occasion.

Jane's Persimmon Pudding

1/2 cup	melted butter		1	cup	persimmon pulp
1/2 cup	chopped walnuts or pecans		2	tsp	baking soda, dissolved in
1 cup	sugar		2	tbs	warm water
2	eggs		3	tbs	brandy
1 cup	flour		1	tsp	vanilla
1/4 tsp	salt		1	cup	currants or chopped raisins
1 tsp	cinnamon				

Mix sugar, butter, walnuts and eggs.
Add flour, salt, cinnamon.
Add persimmon pulp, soda/water, brandy, vanilla and currants.

Thoroughly oil 8-cup steam mold and coat with sugar. Fill 2/3 full with batter. (A 2-lb. coffee can with aluminum foil lid will substitute.)

Place covered mold on rack in a larger pot (rack may be made of pencils or jar lids). Add water to level halfway up mold and cover larger pot. Steam pudding 2-1/2 to 3 hours (longer cooking won't harm it). Finished pudding will be dark, springy and may pull slightly away from mold.

To unmold, turn upside down on a plate. If pudding does not drop right out, shake and pound mold vigorously, right side up, and invert it again. Next alternative is to leave pudding inverted on plate to drop out when cool. Last resort is to loosen pudding with a flat knife. If pudding breaks, it can usually be reassembled.

Pudding may be frozen. To store at room temperature, pour up to 2 tbsp. of brandy over cooled pudding and wrap it tightly in plastic wrap. Add brandy occasionally if it is to be stored for a long time.

Heat pudding before serving and flame at table with brandy. Serve with ice cream or hard sauce.

Hard Sauce: Mix together and then chill

1	cube	unsalted butter, softened
1/2	cup	powdered sugar
2	tbs	brandy
		fresh grated nutmeg to taste

THE SHARPER IMAGE®

650 Davis Street
San Francisco, CA 94111
(415) 445-6000
Telex: 176390 SHARPERIMAGE

Richard Thalheimer
President

PASTA E FAGGIOLI

1 can White Cannellini Beans (Progresso), drained

1 large onion, chopped

2 garlic buds, minced

1 cup dry pasta, small shells

1 can chicken broth

1 bay leaf

½ teaspoon oregano

½ teaspoon basil

2 tablespoons tomato paste

1 large can tomatoes, cut-up

1 tablespoon olive oil

Saute onion and garlic in olive oil. Add all other ingredients
except pasta. Simmer for 15 minutes. Then cook pasta and
drain. Add cooked pasta. Serve with grated Parmesan cheese.
Serves 4

This menu is easy to prepare, and is also healthy.

Richard Thalheimer

ART

Cepes Kirsty

2 large cepes (boletus edulis, or porcini)
enough small new or (birch...) potatoes
         to fill a pyrex dish
2 medium size onions
1 pint of heavy cream
butter
salt & pepper

    butter pyrex dish
    slice potatoes, cepes & onions <u>very thin</u>
    layer them: potato
                onion
                cepe
                potato
                onion
                cepe
salt & pepper & drops of butter in between.

Cover with cream & bake in 350° oven
for half an hour.

— Angie Thieriot

A MOULD of SWEETBREADS
WITH ALBUFERA SAUCE

Preparation for 4 Persons:

450 grams of fresh sweetbreads
1 carrot
1 onion
2 celery sticks
2 or 3 garlic cloves
1 bouquet garni
1 litre veal stock
salt and pepper
Dash of cognac

Chicken Mousse

200 grams of chicken meat, cubed and denerved
2 slices of white bread soaked in milk
30 centilitres of creme fraiche
juice of truffles and chopped truffles

Sauce Albufera

10 centilitres of cognac
10 centilitres of madeira
½ litre of chicken stock
3/4 litre of cream
Dash of truffle juice
100 grams of duck liver (cooked in terrine)
Salt and pepper

Braising of Sweetbreads

Blanch the sweetbreads, refresh and de-nerve. Cut the
vegetables in a mirepoix, brown them quickly in butter,
then add the sweetbreads, deglasser with a little cognac,
moisten with veal stock, season with salt and pepper, cook
for 30 to 40 minutes. Let the sweetbreads cool in their
braising juice. Finally slice in nice Rondelles and
reserve.

847 Montgomery Street San Francisco 94133 (415) 397-5969

Chicken Mousse

Place the chicken meat, salt and pepper in a cutter and chop finely. Add the milk soaked breadcrumbs. Mix again and add cream. Finally put in a touch of truffle juice and the chopped truffles. Reserve.

Composition of the Dish

Take a souffle dish 2" high and 3 3/4 round, butter mould, garnish bottom with sweetbread slices, add a little of chicken mousse and finish with a few slices of sweetbreads. Cook in a Bain-Marie in moderate oven at 325°. When cooked, take out of mould and place on a plate covered with Sauce Albufera.

At "Ernie's" we serve the "Gateau" of Sweetbreads with chanterelles, tiny root vegetables and a scallop of fresh duck liver lightly sauteed and garnish with fresh chervil.

Albufera Sauce

Reduce cognac and madeira to half, add chicken stock, reduce again by half, add cream and reduce once more to the consistency of a light sauce. Season carefully, thicken with the puree of foie gras and finish off with a touch of truffle juice. Serve <u>very</u> hot!

Bruno Tison

847 Montgomery Street San Francisco 94133 (415) 397-5969

ANTHONY S. TIANO
PRESIDENT AND
CHIEF EXECUTIVE OFFICER

KQED 9
KQEC 32
KQED-FM 88.5
SAN FRANCISCO FOCUS MAGAZINE
GOLDEN GATE PRODUCTIONS

500 EIGHTH STREET
SAN FRANCISCO, CALIFORNIA 94103
415 864-2000

SAN FRANCISCO CELEBRITY CHEFS COOKBOOK

Recipe for Pizza

Crust
- Dissolve 2 packages of dry granulated yeast (if you use 3 packages, it will rise faster) in 2 cups warm water
- Stir in 1 cup flour and let "work" while you mix the rest
- Cream 2 sticks of soft margarine and 1 cup of sugar
- Beat in 4 eggs--one at a time
- Stir in 2 tsps. salt
- Stir in 2 cups flour
- Add part of the yeast/flour mix
- Add more yeast/flour mix
- Add 2 more cups flour
- Add rest of yeast/flour mix
- Add 1 more cup flour

Flour a bread board and knead it for 10 minutes. Oil a large bowl and put dough in it, turning it over to lightly cover the whole ball.

Set bowl in a warm place covered with a cloth until it doubles in size.

Sauce
- 3 cans tomato paste
- 3 cans tomato sauce
- 2 cups water
- Italian seasoning
- 1/4 cup sugar
- Seasoning salt & pepper
- Parsley flakes
- Oregano

Buy 4 packages sliced mozzarella cheese

Roll dough out very thin--put a little oil on the foil to ease shaping

Layer dough, mozzarella, sauce, then pepperoni or green chili, then parmesan or romano grated cheese

Bake at 375° for 15-20 minutes or until it is brown and bubbly*

*If freezing, bake for 10-12 minutes, then freeze. To reheat, bake frozen at 425° for 10-15 minutes.

Serves millions

WALTER G. TOLLESON

musical organization, inc.

1815 TARAVAL
SAN FRANCISCO
CALIFORNIA 94116
Phone (415) 665-4000

NOVEMBER 4, 1986

THE "MEXICAN DISH"
(IT'S NOT HAUTE CUISINE, BUT IT SURE TASTES GOOD)

INGREDIENTS FOR TWO:
1/2-3/4 LB. OF GROUND BEEF
HEAD LETTUCE
TOMATO (CHERRY TOMATOES ARE THE EASIEST TO SLICE)
GREEN ONIONS (3)
CELERY STALKS (2)
CHEDDAR CHEESE SLICES (2)
TORTILLA CHIPS
SALSA SAUCE (WHICHEVER WAY YOU LIKE IT, MEDIUM OR HOT)
CHILI WITH BEANS (I PREFER DENNISON'S HOT CHILE WITH BEANS)

PREPARATION:
FORM FOUR EQUAL-SIZE GROUND BEEF PATTIES.
SLICE ONIONS, TOMATOES, CELERY AND LETTUCE AND PUT IN INDIVIDUAL
  PILES ON A SERVING PLATE AND PUT ON DINNER TABLE.
PUT TORTILLA CHIPS IN A MOUND ON THE DINNER PLATES.
BROIL OR FRY THE BEEF PATTIES. WHEN YOU TURN THEM OVER PUT
  CHEDDAR CHEESE SLICES ON THE PATTIES.
COOK THE CHILI WITH BEANS SO THAT IT WILL BE VERY HOT WHEN YOU
  FINISH COOKING THE GROUND ROUND.

WHEN THROUGH COOKING:
PUT THE PATTIES ON TOP OF THE TORTILLA CHIPS YOU HAVE ALREADY PUT
ON THE DINNER PLATES.
PUT THE CHILI WITH BEANS ON TOP OF THE PATTIES.

AFTER SERVING IT IS UP TO THE INDIVIDUAL TO ADD THE VEGETABLES
(THE ONIONS, TOMATOES, CELERY AND LETTUCE) AND THE SALSA.

THE BIG TRICK IS GET EVERYTHING READY FOR THE DINERS SO THEY
CAN PUT ON THE VEGETABLES AND SALSA WHEN THE CHILI AND MEAT ARE
STILL HOT.
WARNING

THIS DISH IS HABIT-FORMING.

ENJOY!

"SEÑOR" WALT TOLLESON

SAN FRANCISCO BALLET

455 Franklin Street San Francisco, California 94102 (415) 861-5600

Helgi Tomasson
Artistic Director

ICELANDIC CREAM DESSERT

4 egg yolks
4 tbs confectioners sugar
1½ cups heavy cream - whipped
1 tsp lemon juice
1 can of pears - drained & diced
2 or 3 bananas - diced
grated chocolate

1) Beat egg yolks and sugar together
2) Fold in whipped cream
3) Add lemon juice
4) Fold in diced bananas and pears
Cover top with grated chocolate

"This has always been a favorite of our family, I hope it will
be a favorite of yours."

HELGI TOMASSON

194

150 REDWOOD, SAN FRANCISCO, CALIFORNIA 94102, 415 · 861 · 7827

FISH PAILLARD WITH GINGER, GARLIC AND TOMATOES

What black bean cake did for the Santa Fe Bar & Grill in Berkeley, this paillard of fish did for Stars in San Francisco. I developed it with the same purpose: to have at the opening of a restaurant a fast, new, easily cooked, and easily understood dish. It was an instant hit, and can be with you at home. With a little advance chopping and slicing, you have a winner in five minutes. I call this dish a "paillard" because the piece of fish is cut like a paillard of veal-in a very thin slice and pounded even thinner, to use James Beard's words. It is so thin that you do not have to use a pan to cook the fish, and that is why you can't overcook it. The heat of the plate and the hot sauce poured over the paillard will do all the cooking. The original recipe had lobster butter drizzled over it, and since then it has also featured fresh chilies, Chinese black beans, and most of the other ingredients that recur throughout this book.

4 two-ounce slices	salmon, tuna, halibut, grouper, red snapper, sturgeon, sea bass, or albacore, skinned, boneless; no thicker than ¼ inch
6 tablespoons	butter
	salt and freshly ground pepper
1 cup	fish stock (page 218)
2-ounce piece	fresh ginger, peeled, finely chopped
3 cloves	garlic, finely chopped
2/3 cup	tomato concasse
12 sprigs	fresh cilantro

Serves 4

Heat the broiler or oven.
Pound the fish slices until they are evenly 1/8 inch thick. Spread 4 heat-resistant plates with ½ teaspoon of the butter each.
Put the plates in the oven or under the broiler until hot. Season the paillards with salt and pepper and put 1 on each plate. Mix the fish stock, ginger, garlic, and tomato in a saute pan. Bring to a boil and cook 2 minutes. Whisk the remaining butter into the saute pan. Turn the pieces of fish over on the plates and pour the sauce over the fish. By the time you garnish the plates with cilantro, the fish will be done.

Jeremiah Tower's New American Classics
Harper & Row Publishers
Fall 1986

Mrs. John R. Upton
2440 Pacific Avenue
San Francisco, California 94115

Herring-Roe Casserole

Fresh or tinned herring roe placed lengthwise in a buttered pyrex
dish and covered with the following sauce:

1 cup heavy cream
1 tbs. butter
2 tbs. flour
1 tsp. anchovy paste

1 tsp. Worcestershire sauce
1 tbs. catsup
paprika and pepper to taste

Make a sauce of these ingredients and pour over the fish roe.
Bake in the oven just long enough to brown. Serve at once.
I always double the recipe and serve rice in a separate dish.
As the herring roe is not easy to find, I write to either
Harrods or Fortnum and Mason in London to order a case sent out
from there.

This recipe was first prepared by the Food and Wine Society of
London before World War II.

Mrs. John R. Upton
Vice President
San Francisco Ballet Board of Trustees

COQUILLES SAINT-JACQUES A L'ORANGE ET SAFRAN

(Sea Scallops with Orange and Saffron)

1 pound fresh sea scallops
   (approximately 16 pieces to a pound)
1 orange
1 tomato, skinned, seeded, and diced
½ teaspoon saffron threads
1 teaspoon butter
1 small shallot, chopped
2 tablespoons dry white wine
¼ cup cream
2 tablespoons chopped parsley
Salt and pepper to taste

1. Slice each scallop in thirds or ¼ inch thick.
    Place in a bowl.

2. Grate orange skin, being careful not to include the
    white pith, which is bitter. Squeeze juice and pour
    into bowl with scallops. Add grated peel, diced tom-
    atoes, saffron, salt, and pepper. Marinate for 3-4
    hours or longer in refrigerator.

3. Strain scallops; reserve marinade. Put butter and
    shallots in saute pan, add scallops, and saute for
    1 minute - be careful not to overcook to retain flavor
    and tenderness. Remove scallops, add white wine,
    marinade for scallops, and cream. Reduce by one half.

4. Return scallops to pan, bring to boil, and transfer
    immediately to serving dish. Sprinkle with parsley.

Serves four persons. This recipe could be served as an
appetizer or as a first course. Excellent served with
fresh linguini.

890 Chestnut Street
San Francisco, Ca. 94133
Tel no. 415 673 7094

Ice Box Cake

Fill sides and bottom of a deep pan with lady
fingers. Pour in a sauce made as follows:

> 1 tbsp. sugar
> 6 tbsp. sweet chocolate
> 4 tbsp. water.

Bring mixture to a boil. While it is hot,
beat in four egg yolks. Beat 4 egg whites until
stiff. Add half to sauce, then fold in the
other half. Cover the mixture with more lady
fingers and place in ice box over night. Cover
with whipped cream two hours before serving.

This recipe was given to me by my late mother-
in-law, Blanche Walker, who lived in Kula, Maui.
In the early nineteen hundreds, ladies in Hawaii
pretended it was declassé to cook. Actually many
of them were excellent cooks and they taught
their young Japanese servants to cook and serve.

Misa, Mrs. Walker's Japanese girl, had a footnote
to this recipe. It is better to put the ice box
cake in the freezer until it is frozen, or to
leave it in a very cold ice box for two days
before serving it.

Dorothea
Walker

KPIX 5

855 BATTERY STREET ☐ SAN FRANCISCO CA 94111-1597 ☐ 415 362-5550   WESTINGHOUSE BROADCASTING AND CABLE INC

WAYNE WALKER
Sports Director

This recipes is an original from our friend,
Sarah Boling. It's so simple, I've cooked
it for 20 and have received rave reviews!

Ah, a rave review...something everyone in my
business always craves!

      ANGEL HAIR PASTA W/ CILANTRO,
    SUN-DRIED TOMATOES & FETA CHEESE

8 oz. sun-dried tomatoes coarsely chopped,
      + approximately 2 Tbls. olive oil,
      in which they are packed

8 oz. feta cheese, crumbled
1 bunch fresh cilantro, coarsely chopped
4 oz. angel hair pasta, cooked

Combine first 3 ingredients and set aside.
Cook pasta according to directions and toss
with the tomatoes, cilantro and feta cheese.
Serve warm or cold.

Serves four as a side dish.

Enjoy

Wayne Walker

:CHEZ:PANISSE:
:: CAFE:&:RESTAURANT ::
:: 1517:SHATTUCK:BERKELEY:94709 ::
:: 548·5525 ::

Buckwheat Crepes with Plum Jelly

To make about 1 quart batter, enough for 32 crepes 6 inches in diameter:

2 cups milk

¼ teaspoon salt

½ teaspoon sugar

4 Tablespoons unsalted butter

¼ cup plus 1 Tablespoon buckwheat flour, to which add regular flour
   to give 1¼ cups flour in all

1 Tablespoon vegetable oil

3 eggs

½ cup beer

Heat the milk, salt, sugar, and butter until the butter has
melted. Measure the flour into a mixing bowl, make a well in it,
put in the oil, and break in the whole eggs. Mix slightly with
a whisk or an electric hand mixer to incorporate some of the flour.
When it starts to thicken, add the warm milk mixture, little by little,
beating it well until smooth. When you have added a little over
1 cup of milk, or enough to make a medium-thick batter, continue
to beat until it is quite smooth, adding the rest of the milk
mixture gradually. Mix in the beer and strain into a refrigerator
container. Chill the batter for at least 2 hours before frying.
The batter will keep for five days to a week with no problem.
The crepes can also be fried several hours before you want to use
them, then kept covered.

To fry the crepes: Let the batter warm slightly. So that the crepes
are very thin and delicate, heat your crepe pan until a drop of
water sizzles when you throw it in the pan. You may rub the pan
with butter and wipe it out with a paper towel to keep the first
crepe from sticking; you won't need to do it again. Lift the pan
off the heat and ladle about 2 Tablespoons of the batter into the
center of the pan. (Measure 2 Tablespoons of water into your ladle
to see how full you will want it when you dip up the batter.) There
shouldn't be any more batter than will stick to the bottom of the
pan in a thin layer when you pour it in.

Tilt and rotate the pan immediately to make the batter run around
the edge and cover and rest of the bottom evenly, then set the pan
back on the heat. The batter should bubble when it hits the pan
and make little holes that go all the way through the crepe. Brown
the first side- it takes about a minute over a medium flame. If the
edge browns too fast, run a silver knife around the edge of the
pan to loosen just the thin edge of the crepe so it will be pulled
away from the pan and won't burn while the rest is browning.

:CHEZ:PANISSE:
:: CAFE:&:RESTAURANT ::
:: 1517:SHATTUCK:BERKELEY:94709 ::
:: 598·5525 ::

Buckwheat Crepes
-2-

Lift the crepe and turn it over with your hands. Cook the second
side for about 1 minute also and turn out on a piece of plastic
wrap. The side that browns first is the right side of the crepe
and should be brown and lacy.

Fold crepes in half and place on a lightly buttered baking sheet.
Bake in a hot oven 3 or 4 minutes, until they are warm through.
Remove the crepes from the oven, drizzle with a little unsalted
butter and fold into quarters. Spread with plum jelly and serve.

Note. To serve four, you may prepare half this recipe, for 16 crepes.

GAZPACHO ANDALUZ

½ LB. FRESH, RED TOMATOES

2 PIMENTOS, GREEN FRESH - USE CANNED IF UNAVAILABLE

1 LARGE GARLIC TOOTH

4 TBS. RED WINE VINEGAR
6 TBS. OLIVE OIL
5 OZ. DRIED BREAD CRUMBS - NO CRUSTS
SALT TO TASTE

PEEL TOMATOES, SLICE PIMENTOS, CHOP GARLIC. SOAK
CRUMBS WITH VINEGAR, OIL + SALT. BLEND ALL,
MAKING A PURÉE. ADD 2 to 2½ PTS. WATER, LESS
IF QUICK CHILL DESIRED AND ICE CUBES ARE ADDED.

SERVE VERY COLD GARNISHED GENEROUSLY WITH DICED PEPPER
TOMATOES, ONION, CROUTONS.

This recipe came from friends in
Pamplona after they received their
first American blender in 1956.

Ian White

202

WILLIAMS-SONOMA

• WILLIAMS-SONO
• HOLD EVERYTH
• GARDENER'S EL

100 North Point Str
San Francisco, CA 9
415/421-7900
Telex: 6713712 Cuisine

Charles E. Williams
Chairman of the Board

POACHED SALMON IN FOIL

4 medium sized fresh salmon steaks, 1" thick
1 or 2 carrots, peeled and thinly sliced
1 or 2 lemons, very thinly sliced
4 to 6 green onions, trimmed and sliced or coarsely chopped

Dried ground dill weed
Sea salt
Freshly ground pepper

Preheat oven to 425°

Cut 4 pieces of aluminum foil 12" x 12".
In the center of each sheet of the foil arrange 6-8 slices of
carrot (covering an area approximately the size of one of the
salmon steaks). Add 1-2 slices of lemon (depending on size)
on top of carrots, sprinkle with the sliced or chopped green
onion and 1 or 2 pinches of dill. Place a salmon steak on
top of each and repeat process of carrots, lemon, onion and
dill. Season top with sea salt and pepper.

Make a packet of the aluminum foil by bringing two sides
together and folding over twice. Flatten ends and fold over
corners, then fold over ends, press tightly and turn up so
they are well sealed. Place on a baking sheet and bake in
center of oven for 15-20 minutes.

At end of 15 minutes test the flesh of one steak with a fork.
Inside should be just cooked (not raw). Do not overbake.

Open packets, peel off skin around edge of salmon, leaving
carrots, etc. Serve immediately with a cooked green vegetable.
Pour any juice accumulated in foil packet over the salmon.

Serves 4.

This is a very simple way to prepare salmon
or other fish that is not too oily.

CHICKEN ALMOND

4 Broiler halves or quartered Chicken parts

2 medium yellow onions, thinly sliced

1 cup soy sauce

1-1/2 cups brown sugar, firmly packed

1/2 cup sherry - dry or medium

1/2 lb. mushrooms, thinly sliced

2 - 2-1/2 oz. packages sliced almonds

1 cup butter

Pepper to taste

Ground ginger to taste

Paprika

Rub broilers well with pepper, paprika and ground ginger. Do not use any salt. Brown chicken under broiler well. Saute onions in butter until golden, add soy sauce, brown sugar and sherry. Mix together well. Place browned chicken, skin side up in casserole, cover with onions and all mushrooms and almonds. Cover chicken with all ingredients and cook at 300° for 45 minutes, tightly covered. If necessary, raise heat to 325° and bake 15 more minutes.

When Henry Kissinger was Secretary of State, I served as one of two architect members on the U.S. Delegation to the United Nation's Conference on Human Settlements or "Habitat" as it was called, in Vancouver, Canada. A friend loaned me their spectacular penthouse adjacent to Stanley Park in downtown Vancouver and close to the conference center. In cooperation with the U. S. Delegation staff and the assistance of Margaret Mead, a great organizer and people person, and her friends, Bucky Fuller and Barbara Ward (Lady Jackson), I hosted a number of back to back luncheons and dinner parties. This was my best recipe as it could be easily extended for unexpected guests and was a useful leftover. And it tasted great.

WENDELL W. WITTER
101 CALIFORNIA STREET
P. O. BOX 7597
SAN FRANCISCO, CA 94120

Light luncheon sandwich:
Toast four slices whole
wheat bread on one side.

On untoasted side spread
Underwood deviled ham,
 (1 can for 4 slices)
Place slice of beef-steak tomato
on spread deviled ham.
Top with slice of sharp
cheddar cheese.

Place under broiler until
cheese bubbles,
Serve with iced tea or
cold beer.
        Enjoy!
            Wendell Witter

44 Montgomery Street
San Francisco, California 94104-4602
(415) 393-4300
Telex: 340336

PINEAPPLE-UPSIDE DOWN CAKE

Part I
   1/3 cup butter
   1 cup brown sugar
   3 slices canned pineapple
   Maraschino cherries

Part II
   3 eggs, separated
   1 cup granulated sugar
   1 cup flour (Swans Down)
   1 tsp. baking powder
   1/4 tsp. salt
   1/3 cup pineapple juice

Melt butter in bottom of deep 9-inch black iron skillet. Add sugar and stir until melted. Remove from heat, place a whole slice of pineapple in center with half slices around it and cherries.

Beat egg whites stiff and gradually fold in sugar. Set aside. Beat egg yolks well. Add sifted flour, baking powder and salt. Blend well. Gradually add hot pineapple juice to mixture and blend well. Fold this mixture carefully into beaten egg whites. Pour batter over fruit.

Bake in moderate oven of 350° for 35-45 minutes.

Remove from oven, let stand two minutes and turn cake upside down onto cake platter.

Happy Eating,

Dennis Wu
Partner

YanCan

INTERNATIONAL
COOKING SCHOOL

This is one of my favorite recipes. It's simple, easy and can be prepared ahead of time. Great for parties and picnics. The well-balanced sweet and sour flavor will guarantee to be your family's favorite.

CITRUS-SPICED SPARERIBS

Makes: 4 servings
Cooking time: 24 minutes

1½ to 2 pounds pork spareribs

MARINADE
   3 tablespoons each soy sauce
     and dry sherry
   ¼ teaspoon each Chinese five-
     spice and salt

   1 egg, lightly beaten
 1/3 cup all-purpose flour

   Vegetable oil, for deep-
   frying

BRAISING SAUCE
   2 teaspoons vegetable oil
   ½ teaspoon minced fresh ginger
   2 shallots, minced
 1/3 cup fresh orange juice
   ¼ cup each frozen tangerine
     juice concentrate and
     fresh lemon juice
   3 tablespoons packed brown
     sugar
   2 tablespoons fresh lime
     juice
   2 teaspoons grated lemon peel
   1 teaspoon cornstarch mixed
     with 2 teaspoons water

   Orange wedges, for garnish

PREPARATION

Trim and discard excess fat from spareribs, then cut ribs apart between bones. Combine marinade ingredients in a large bowl. Add spareribs, stirring to coat all sides. Cover and refrigerate for at least 4 hours or overnight.

Drain ribs briefly. Dip ribs in egg, then coat evenly with flour, shaking off excess. Set on a plate and let stand for 10 minutes.

COOKING

Set wok in a ring stand and add oil to a depth of 1½ to 2 inches. Place over medium-high heat until oil reaches about 350°F. Add spareribs, 4 or 5 pieces at a time, and deep-fry turning occasionally, for about 8 minutes or until golden brown. Lift out and drain on paper towels. Cook remaining ribs.

Meanwhile, place a wide frying pan over medium-high heat until hot. Add oil, swirling to coat sides. Add ginger and shallots; cook, stirring, until fragrant. Add remaining braising sauce ingredients and cook, stirring, until sauce boils and thickens slightly. Reduce heat and add ribs to pan. Simmer, uncovered, over medium-low heat, turning ribs occasionally, for about 5 minutes or until ribs are well coated. Garnish with orange wedges and serve hot.

TIPS:

For handy bite-size hors d'oeuvres, ask your butcher to cut across the ribs into 2-inch strips.

*Note: Recipe by Martin Yan of The Yan Can Cook show on public television.

Mr. Ira Yeager

at Home

CHICKEN IN A SINK FOR 50 OR "SINKED CHICKEN"

Pat Steger sez: 'At his dinner the chicken was served in the kitchen sink.' The sink is a beautiful porcelain Sherle Wagner hand-painted sink used as a tureen!

100 skinned chicken thighs (at one party the char burned out the electric disposal with the 100 skins)
4 big white cabbage heads, chopped
2 jars Dijon mustard
2 c. water
1 jar capers
1 container sour cream
parsley

Place cabbage, mustard and water in a giant pot. Cook on medium hot gas or electric burner until cooked. Drain and reduce liquid. Throw in capers and sour cream. Mix up and serve in "the kitchen sink." Garnish with chopped parsley. (In the old Powell Street studio before I had a stove, this was cooked in a Dutch oven on top of a standing gas heater!).

Stephen Zellerbach

1914 Polk Street
San Francisco CA 94109
415 441 7384

ORANGE GLAZED PORK ROAST

3-5 pound boneless shoulder or boneless loin roast

3/4 cup orange marmalade   1/2 teaspoon onion salt

2 tablespoons lemon juice   1/2 teaspoon celery salt

2 tablespoons soy sauce   1/2 teaspoon white pepper

1 tablespoon rubbed sage

2 oz. Calvados or Grand Marnier or 4 oz. Apple Jack

   Rub roast with sage, two salts and pepper. Add more if
necessary to cover. Bake in 350° oven approximately two hours to
170° on meat thermometer. Mix together and add the remaining
ingredients for the last 1/2 hour. After removing the roast, the
gravy may be thickened, if needed, with corn starch.

   This roast is wonderful if served with pureed chestnuts and
brussel sprouts, for those who like either or both.

RECIPE INDEX

SAN FRANCISCO'S

CELEBRITY CHEFS

Sponsored by
THE MONTEREY VINEYARD
Proceeds to benefit
THE SAN FRANCISCO BALLET
•
Sam Bronfman and The San Francisco Ballet

If you would like to support the San Francisco Ballet by ordering additional copies, send:

$9.95 per copy plus $1.50 for postage and handling fee (2 or more books, $2.50 postage and handling). Washington State residents must add 7.9% sales tax.

Please send me ___ copies

BILL TO:

Name _____

Address _____

City _____ State ____ Zip _____

SHIP TO:

Name _____

Address _____

City _____ State ____ Zip _____

☐ Payment enclosed   ☐ Charge

Visa # _____ Exp. Date _____

MasterCard # _____ Exp. Date _____

Signature _____ • _____

PEANUT BUTTER PUBLISHING

329 - 2nd Avenue W. ▪ Seattle, WA 98119 ▪ (206) 281-5965
1- 800 - 426 - 5537